CROSS STITCH
Myth & Magic

CROSS STITCH
Myth & Magic

David and Charles

A DAVID & CHARLES BOOK

David & Charles is a subsidiary of F+W (UK) Ltd.,
an F+W Publications Inc. company

First published in the UK in 2002
Reprinted 2003 (three times)
First paperback edition 2005

Distributed in North America
by F+W Publications, Inc.
4700 East Galbraith Road
Cincinnati, OH 45236
1-800-289-0963

ISBN 0 7153 1221 9 hardback
ISBN 0 7153 2210 9 paperback

Designed and produced by Penny & Penny
Printed in China by SNP Leefung for David & Charles
Brunel House   Newton Abbot   Devon

Visit our website at www.davidandcharles.co.uk

David & Charles books are available from all good bookshops;
alternatively you can contact our Orderline on (0)1626 334555 or write to us at
FREEPOST EX2 110, David & Charles Direct, Newton Abbot, TQ12 4ZZ
(no stamp required UK mainland).

Contents

Introduction

This cross stitch book will take you on a journey to the mystical world of Fantasy. Here you will find projects spun from the daydreams of their designers: some based on myth, and some on legend, but most mixed together like a magician's spell with a pinch of reality, a spoonful of romance, and a cupful of imagination. Six exciting chapters are packed with magical designs of castles, wizards, dragons and angels. Within each chapter you will find a showcase design, a medium design for a picture or wallhanging, and a range of smaller projects for cards, box tops and towel edgings. In the first chapter, *Myth & Magic*, the showcase project is by fantasy designer Teresa Wentzler: a stunning study of a princess walking with her dragon. You will also find a wallhanging of Merlin the wizard, and card designs of a castle and a dragon. In *Winter Enchantment* the showcase project of Santa on horseback is designed by Susan

Penny; a frost fairy and winter angel, plus a range of smaller designs complete this wintry chapter. *Oriental Fantasy* takes you on a trip to the mystic East, where you will find the beautiful goddess of mercy, and a colourful oriental dragon. The showcase project in *Angelic Messengers* is the angel of peace, which has been designed by Mary Stockett. Other projects in this chapter include a unicorn and cherubs. In *The Mystic Deep*, Susan Penny has taken her inspiration for *Aquamarine* from an original painting by fantasy artists Linda and Roger Garland. Finally Greek architecture has given Sue Cook the idea for the wallhanging in *Celestial Heaven*: a study of the twelve zodiac signs, where the project can be stitched as a whole or the star signs made into cards or gifts. Truly a magnificent design, and a great way to finish a book that brings dreams to life, and conjures up magic with every stitch.

Myth & Magic

*A*s children we hear stories of magical castles, of princes rescuing beautiful princesses from their evil step-fathers, and of knights in shining armour fighting for the hand of the king's daughter. We hear about the legends of King Arthur and the knights of the Round Table, and of Merlin the wizard who used his special magic powers to help King Arthur rule the land.

As we grow up we start to wonder about the truth behind those stories and legends; we read history books about people who really did live in castles, knights in shining armour who did fight in tournaments, and kings so powerful that humble subjects cowered at the mention of their name.

So in this chapter titled Myth & Magic we celebrate those days gone by; and whether you believe in dragons, King Arthur or Merlin really doesn't matter because each design has a sprinkling of magic that is sure to make you want to pick up your needle and start stitching

The Princess and the Dragon

A beautiful princess walks with her pet dragon. He playfully runs around his mistress, then stretches his wings and waits for her to gently pat his scaly head.
Designed by Teresa Wentzler

❊ *Antique white evenweave, 28 count 26.75x30cm (10¹/₂x11³/₄in)*

❊ *DMC stranded cotton (floss) in the colours listed in the key*

❊ *Tapestry needle, No 26*

❊ *Sharp sewing needle*

❊ *Mill Hill glass seed beads – gold 02011; cobalt blue 00358; ice blue 02006; heather 02025; mauve 02024*

❊ *Gold picture frame*

Stitching the dragon

1 Mark the centre of your fabric with tacking stitches and oversew around the edges to prevent them fraying. Mount the fabric in a frame.

2 Work the design from the centre out following the chart and key on pages 16, 17, 18 and 19. Use two strands of stranded cotton (floss) for all the cross stitch, working each stitch over two threads of evenweave fabric.

3 Some areas of the design are worked using blended needle. This technique gives the stitches a tweeded appearance, blending two colours together in one stitch. If a symbol in the key has two colour numbers listed against it you will need to thread your needle with one strand of each colour. So on page 16, where colour 522 and colour 523 are listed against one symbol, take one strand of each colour, lay them together and then thread your needle in the normal way. Blended needle is also used for the green half cross stitch below the castle.

Adding the backstitch detail

1 All the backstitch is worked using one strand of stranded cotton (floss), apart from the dragon's eye highlight which is worked in two strands of white.

2 The face detail and hair are worked using the small chart on page 19. The face is backstitched in one strand of brown 420. This colour is also used to backstitch the yellow areas of the dragon's wing, neck and tail; the sash, brooch, crown and detail on the princess; and the outer and inner lines of the border.

3 Use burgundy 3740 to backstitch the mauve areas on the dragon's wing, head and neck.

4 Backstitch the castle, all the white/grey areas on the princess, the mauve edges of her sash and her dress with grey 414.

5 The green areas on the dragon's head and wing, and the flowers in the princess's hand are backstitched using green 3362. Finally backstitch the blue areas on the dragon's wing, neck and tail using blue 792.

Adding the beads

Following the chart on pages 16, 17, 18 and 19 for position, stitch the beads on to the design using a sharp needle and one strand of stranded cotton (floss) in a colour close to the colour of each bead. Five bead colours are used, which are stitched in small groups around the border edge and on the flowers in both the princess's hand and the foreground. To finish the design, carefully wash and then press the stitching on a soft fluffy towel. Stretch the design following the instructions on page 108, or take the stitching to a framer for stretching and framing.

Merlin the Wizard

Merlin the wise old wizard used his magical powers in support of King Arthur and the knights of the Round Table. Here we see Merlin holding a flaming orb, working on a spell. Designed by Maria Diaz

❖ *Navy blue evenweave, 28 count 30x35.5cm (12x14in)*
❖ *DMC stranded cotton (floss) in the colours listed in the key*
❖ *DMC rayon thread in the colours listed in the key*
❖ *DMC metallic divisible thread – gold, silver*
❖ *DMC seed beads – aqua 04959*
❖ *Tapestry needle, No 26*
❖ *Navy blue fabric, 44x58.5cm (23x17in)*
❖ *Iron-on vilene*
❖ *Bright blue cord with tassels*
❖ *Curtain pole with finials*
❖ *Sewing needle and thread*

Stitching the dragon

1 Mark the centre of the navy blue evenweave with tacking stitches and oversew around the edges to prevent them fraying. Mount the fabric in a frame.

2 Use two strands of stranded cotton (floss) or two strands of rayon thread for the cross stitch, and two strands for the half cross stitch. Stitch Merlin from the centre out following the chart and key on pages 20 and 21, and working each stitch over two threads of evenweave. It will help to complete the areas of cross stitch worked in stranded cotton (floss) before you start stitching with the rayon thread. The lining of Merlin's cloak and sleeves; the top and bottom of his staff; his amulets, orb and the inner glow surrounding the flame are worked in rayon thread.

3 The backstitch is worked in one strand of stranded cotton (floss), with one strand of gold being used on the cloak, staff ends, amulets at the neck and wrists, and the flame. The moon and star-shaped markings on the cloak are worked in one strand of gold thread. One strand

of silver thread is used to highlight the sleeves and bottom edges of Merlin's blue cloak. The silver thread is also used to stitch the stars on the background fabric surrounding Merlin. Stitch the aqua coloured seed beads on to Merlin's hand and on the amulet at his neck.

Assembling the wallhanging

1 Use a photocopier to make an enlargement of the template on page 104, increasing the size by 200%. Cut out the paper shape, then lay it on your stitching, making sure Merlin is exactly in the centre. Pin the template on to the fabric, then cut out the shape. Iron vilene on to the reverse side of your backing fabric, then use the paper template to cut out the shape. Lay Merlin face up on a flat surface, on top of this place the backing fabric, vilene side uppermost. Stitch the layers together at the edges, with a 1cm (³/8in) seam allowance, but leaving the top edge open. Turn the wallhanging through to the right side, then press carefully.

2 Fold over the top edge of the wallhanging on to the reverse side to form a channel for the pole. The amount that you turn over at the top will depend on the size of the pole that you are using. Working on the reverse side of the hanging, turn under the raw fabric edges and then stitch along the width of the fabric to hold the channel firmly in place. Make sure the channel remains open at both sides for the pole.

3 Pin, then slip stitch the cord around the edge of the wallhanging, starting at the centre bottom point. To finish the wallhanging thread the curtain pole through the channel at the top.

The Castle and the Dragon

*Backstitch has been used to create a blackwork style pattern on the scales of this dragon and the walls of the castle. Both are quick to stitch, using shades of green and brown.
Designed by Susan Penny*

❋ *Antique white linen, 28 count 18x15cm (7x6in) x 2*
❋ *DMC stranded cotton (floss) in the colours listed in the key*
❋ *Tapestry needle, No 26*
❋ *DMC seed beads – copper 09 898*
❋ *Blank greetings cards x 2*
❋ *Handmade paper*

Stitching the dragon and the castle

1 Mark the centre of your linen with tacking stitches and oversew around the edges to prevent them fraying. Mount the fabric in an embroidery hoop.

2 Following the chart and key on the opposite page, work the cross stitch on the dragon and the castle from the centre out, using two strands of stranded cotton (floss), and working each stitch over two threads of fabric. Complete all the cross stitch before starting the backstitch. The main outline of the dragon is done in two strands of dark green 895, all the other backstitch is done in one strand. On the castle the main outline is done in two strands of dark brown 610, all the other backstitch is done in one strand. Stitch a copper bead to the top of each flag pole on the castle. To make it easier to read the chart some of the backstitch colours have been changed. Use the numbers given in the key to identify the correct colour to be used. Wash and press the stitching following the finishing instructions on page 108.

Assembling the cards

Fray the edges of the fabric, then attach the stitching to the front of a blank greetings card, decorated with a rectangle of handmade paper.

The Castle and the Dragon

DMC stranded cotton (floss)

◎	165	**Backstitch**	
✂	167	⁄ 907	
✚	904	⁄ 946	
U	907	⁄ 3045	
↑	946	⁄ 3046	

Backstitch

⁄ 165

⁄ 167

⁄ 610

⁄ 677

⁄ 895

⁄ 906

⁄ 3047

Beads

◆ *Copper

*V3-09-898
DMC copper seed
beads

The Princess and the Dragon

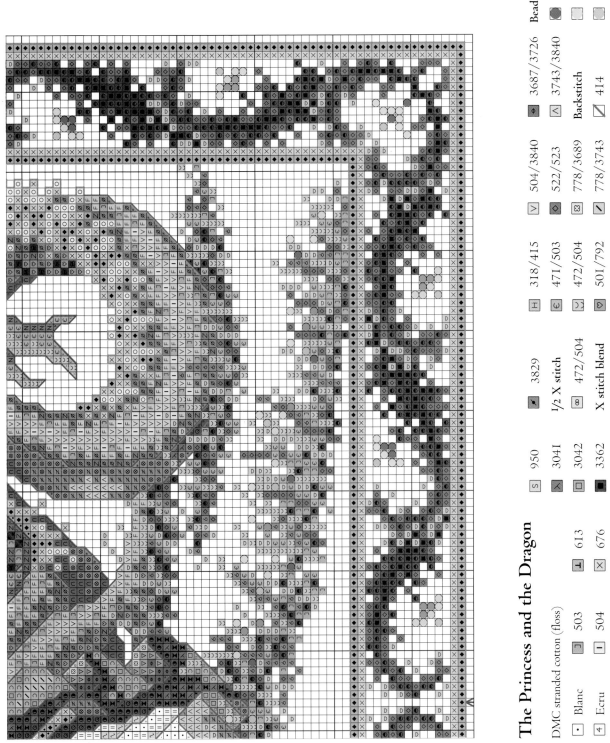

DMC stranded cotton (floss)

·	Blanc	⌐	503	⊣	613	
4	Ecru	I	504	✕	676	
▮	414	⌀	523	○	677	
↗	415	D	524	◆	729	
▦	501	●	610	=	762	
N	502	✳	611	+	792	

◤	950	H	318/415	V	504/3840
⅄	3041	⋴	471/503	◇	522/523
▭	3042	⊃	472/504	⊠	778/3689
▪	3362	◈	501/792	◿	778/3743
◐	3363	▶	501/3346	⊓	792/3740
◑	3740	N	502/3347	◪	3041/3726
⌐	3743	⊗	502/3838	⊗	3041/3838
⊏	3774	▷	503/3839	⊭	3042/3839

3829 — ◨ 3687/3726 — ◍ Φ

½ X stitch — △ 3743/3840

X stitch blend

Backstitch — ◿ 414 / ◿ 420 / ◿ 792 / ◿ 3362 / ◿ 3740

Beads

●	*00358
▫	*02006
◨	*02011
◨	*02024
◨	*02025

*Mill Hill seed beads

Use this small chart for adding the backstitch detail to the face of the princess.

The Princess and the Dragon

DMC stranded cotton (floss)

·	Blanc	⌐	503	⊤	613	S	950	◼	3829	▽	318/415	Φ	3687/3726
4	Ecru	I	504	X	676	⋊	3041		1/2 X stitch	◇	471/503	◇	3743/3840
I	414	⊙	523	○	677	□	3042	8	472/504	⊡	472/504		Backstitch
⟍	415	D	524	◆	729	◼	3362		X stitch blend	⊘	501/792	⟋	414
II	501	●	610	=	762	◐	3363	◓	315/3740	►	501/3346	⟋	420
Z	502	✳	611	+	792	◑	3740	✳	315/3803	N	502/3347	⟋	792
						⟋	3743	C	316/3042	⊗	502/3838	⟋	3362
						L	3774	▷	316/3688	F	503/3839	⟋	3740

▽	504/3840	
◇	522/523	
⊠	778/3689	
⟋	778/3743	
⊓	792/3740	
⋈	3041/3726	
⊗	3041/3838	
⋈	3042/3839	

Beads

●	*00358
◻	*02006
▨	*02011
◻	*02024
◉	*02025

*Mill Hill seed beads

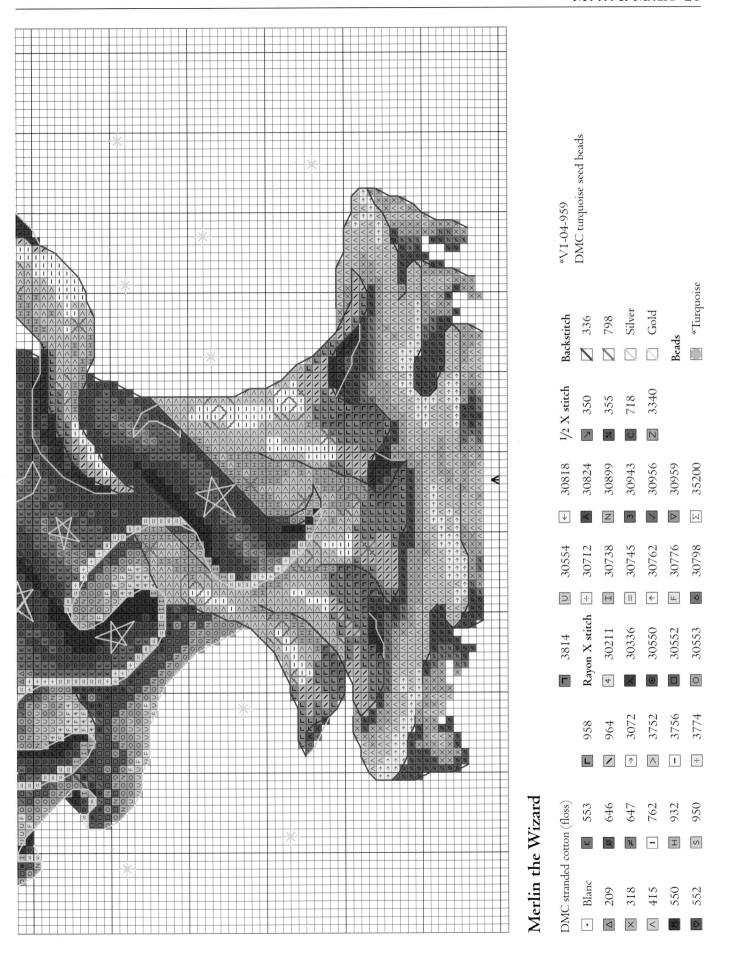

Merlin the Wizard

DMC stranded cotton (floss)

·	Blanc	K	553	⊿	958	
◁	209	⊘	646	⊿	964	
✕	318	⋈	647	→	3072	
⟨	415	−	762	∧	3752	
◼	550	H	932	−	3756	
▷	552	S	950	÷	3774	

◣	3814	U	30554	↓	30818			**Backstitch**	
	Rayon X stitch	÷	30712	▲	30824	╱	336	
4	30211	I	30738	N	30899	╱	798	
✖	30336	=	30745	3	30943	╱	Silver
◉	30550	←	30762	∨	30956	╱	Gold
□	30552	F	30776	▷	30959		**Beads**
O	30553	♂	30798	⅀	35200	⬢	*Turquoise

½ X stitch

↗	350
✖	355
C	718
N	3340

*VI-04-959
DMC turquoise seed beads

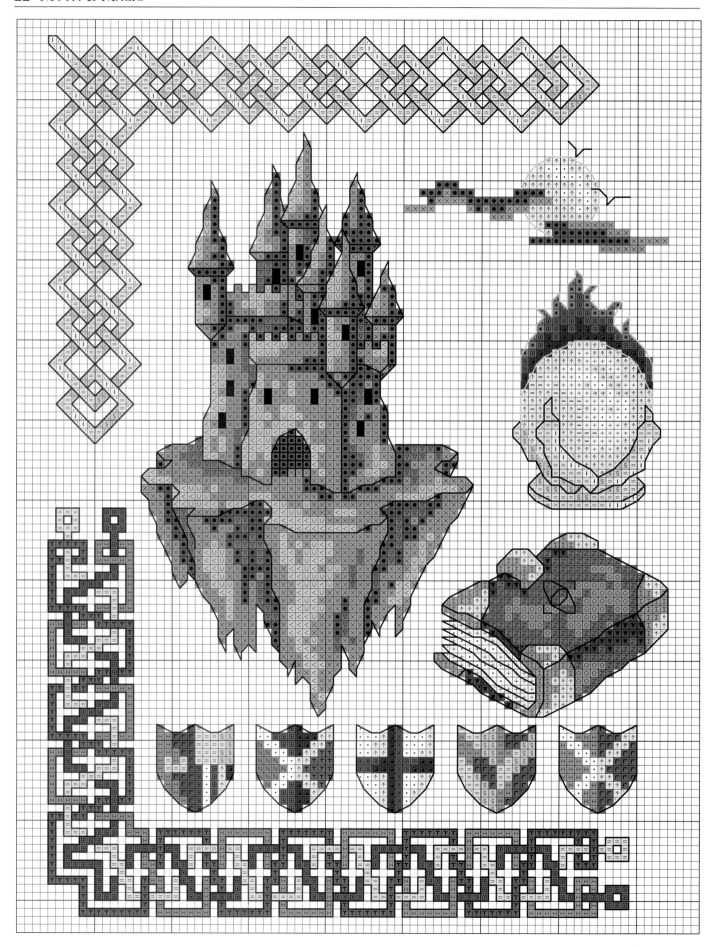

Myth & Magic Motifs

DMC stranded cotton (floss)

·	Blanc	▣	911
→	225	▽	926
■	310	U	928
▣	321	●	931
✕	413	✕	932
⊥	414	4	963
▼	434	N	989
Z	435	↑	3072
O	436	✳	3328
I	648	T	3347
+	712	∩	3354
I	745	S	3820
−	775	=	3822
┏	798	**Backstitch**	
H	799	╱	321
▣	815	╱	844
<	827	╱	*Silver

*Metallic silver thread

Winter Enchantment

At night, when the snow lies crisp and white on the ground and clouds blanket the moon, the landscapes can look very magical. The air is still, and the eerie light of the winter moon turns the snow a ghostly shade of violet. As you watch the landscape you see a slight movement in the trees, a glistening cobweb rocks gently in the moonlight, and an icicle drops suddenly to the ground, shattering into a million tiny pieces. Did you see something move in the trees, or was it just the moonlight playing tricks on your eyes? In this chapter called Winter Enchantment we see three magical winter designs: Santa riding on horseback to an enchanted castle; a frost angel covering the landscape with ice from her long pointed finger; and an angel dressed in wintry robes sitting on the crook of the moon. So the next time you look out on a frosty scene and think you see a movement in the shadows, ask yourself was it your imagination or really a little bit of winter magic being spun before your eyes?

A Stranger Cometh

Santa's journey has been long and difficult. The cold is now penetrating his thick velvet cloak and he begins to shiver. He decides to seek sanctuary in the frozen castle, but will he be welcome?
Designed by Susan Penny

❄ *Cream Aida fabric, 14 count 48x41cm (19x16in)*
❄ *DMC stranded cotton (floss) in the colours listed in the key*
❄ *Tapestry needle, No 24*
❄ *DMC gold divisible thread*
❄ *Seed beads – turquoise and red*
❄ *Gold picture frame*

Stitching the design

1 Mark the centre of your Aida fabric with tacking stitches and oversew around the edges to prevent them fraying. Mount the fabric in a frame or embroidery hoop.

2 Work the design from the centre out following the chart and key on pages 32, 33, 34 and 35. Use two strands of stranded cotton (floss) for the cross stitch, apart from the gold on the horse which is stitched in one strand of gold divisible thread.

3 The border edge which is stitched around the design is made up of two rows of red cross stitch, with a gold backstitch square between. In the centre of each square is a red seed bead.

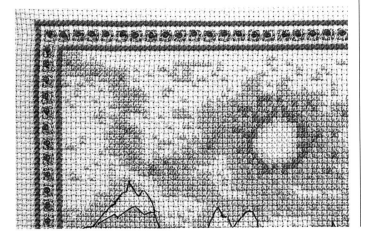

Making the tassel

The tassel on the saddle can be stitched in cross stitch and backstitch, or if you prefer it can be made and then attached on top of the stitching. If you are making the tassel then you will need to use the small section of chart on page 34 to complete the horse where the tassel has been removed. To make the tassel, cut lengths of gold metallic thread 5cm (2in) long. Make a bundle with the threads, then fold them in half. Tie the bundle together just down from the folded edge. Use your needle threaded with gold metallic thread to go through the loop at the top of the tassel, and then attach the tassel to the saddle.

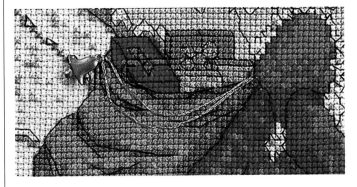

Finishing the design

Backstitch the main areas of the design in one strand of grey 844 stranded cotton (floss), then make a small backstitch to highlight the horse's eye in one strand of white. Use gold metallic thread to stitch squares around the border, and make two long stitches across the top of the sack, leaving the loops hanging loose. Secure the thread with a few small stitches. Sew a bell shaped charm at the back of the sack, over the thread ends. Stitch turquoise beads on to Santa's cloak. Carefully wash, press and then stretch the design following the instructions on page 108, or take the stitching to a framer for stretching and framing.

Frost Fairy

The frost fairy weaves a spell and casts her magic out into the still, cold air. Nothing escapes her powers: trees and hedgerows turn white, and the grass becomes crisp underfoot. Designed by Susan Penny from a painting by Linda and Roger Garland

❊ *Blue linen, 32 count 28x35.5cm (11x14in)*

❊ *DMC stranded cotton (floss) in the colours listed in the key*

❊ *Kreinik blending filament – white100HL*

❊ *Tapestry needle, No 26*

❊ *Seed beads – red and pink for the holly berries; white for the border; glass for the frost fairy*

❊ *Petite beads – glass for frost fairy*

❊ *Silver snowflake charm*

❊ *Silver picture frame*

Stitching the frost fairy

1 Mark the centre of your linen with tacking stitches and oversew around the edges to prevent them fraying. Mount the fabric in a frame or embroidery hoop.

2 Work the design from the centre out following the chart and key on pages 36 and 37. Unless stated below, use two strands of stranded cotton (floss) for the cross stitch, two strands for half cross stitch, and one strand for the backstitch, working each stitch over two threads of fabric.

Backstitching the border

The green border lines are backstitched in three strands of stranded cotton (floss). The snowflakes on the border are worked with two strands of white stranded cotton (floss) and one strand of white blending filament.

Stitching hedgerows

To make the frosty hedgerows, use one strand of stranded cotton (floss), and one strand of white blending filament to make french knots along the darker blue area of the fields in the foreground. Add as many or as few french knots as you feel you need to get the right effect. You may prefer to leave the hedgerows as cross stitch.

Adding the backstitch and beads

1 Use one strand of white stranded cotton (floss) and one strand of white blending filament for all the backstitch on the frost fairy, the trees, and the holly leaves covered in frost. Use one strand of green stranded cotton (floss) and one strand of white blending filament to backstitch the rest of the holly leaves.

2 Following the chart for position, stitch white seed beads to the border snowflakes, and red and pink seed beads to the holly. The glass seed and petite beads on the frost fairy are not shown on the chart, but should be stitched randomly over the backstitch.

Adding a charm

Finally backstitch the snowflake hanging from the fairy's wrist, adding glass seed beads to the points. If you prefer you can use a silver charm in place of the stitched snowflake. If you are using a charm, do not cross stitch the snowflake. Carefully wash and press the stitching, then stretch it following the instructions on page 108, or take it to a framer for stretching and framing.

Winter Angel

A beautiful winter angel rests on the moon. She folds her wings and waits, her long flowing robes falling around her ankles. In her hand she holds a star: a light to guide her on her journey. Designed by Sue Cook

- *Pale blue linen, 28 count 28x35.5cm (11x14in)*
- *DMC stranded cotton (floss) in the colours listed in the key*
- *DMC rayon thread in the colours listed in the key*
- *DMC metallic gold divisible thread*
- *Tapestry needle, No 26*
- *Gold picture frame*

Stitching the angel

1 Mark the centre of your linen with tacking stitches and oversew around the edges to prevent them fraying. Mount the fabric in a frame or embroidery hoop.

2 Work the angel from the centre out following the chart and key on the opposite page. Use two strands of stranded cotton (floss) for the cross stitch and one strand for the backstitch, apart from the angel's dress where one strand of stranded cotton (floss) has been mixed with one strand of rayon. The moon is stitched in half cross stitch in one strand of stranded cotton (floss) mixed with one strand of rayon, then backstitched with one strand of rayon thread 33820 orange.

3 The star in the angel's hand is backstitched in metallic gold thread, before adding yellow french knots.

4 The angel's face, hands and feet are backstitched in one strand of 3064 stranded cotton (floss), her hair in 838 brown, dress in 930 blue, her scarf in 154 burgundy, and her wings in 451 beige.

5 Stretch the stitching following the instructions on page 108, or take it to a framer for stretching and framing.

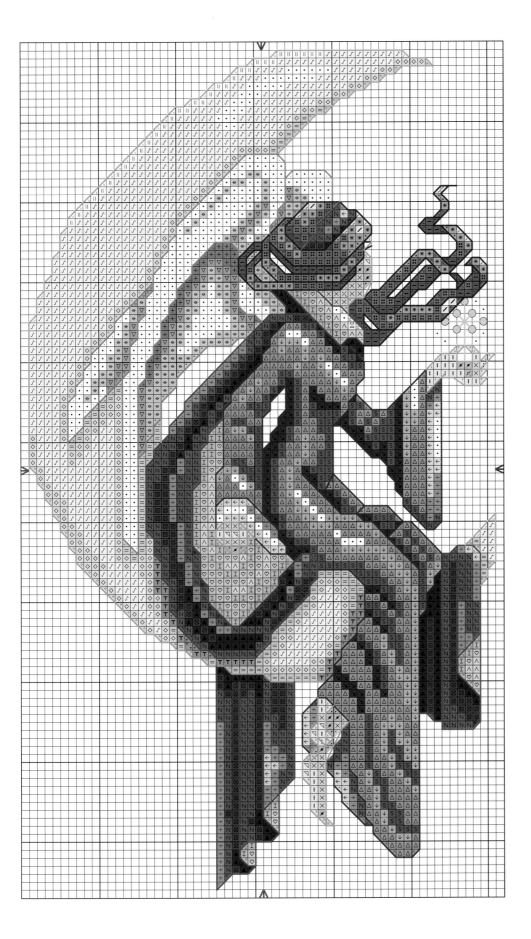

Winter Angel

DMC stranded cotton (floss)

·	Blanc		**X stitch blend**
▲	154	◼	930/*30930
▬	167	S	931/*30931
✳	422	△	932/*30932
+	451	↓	3752/*30762
▽	452		**¹/₂ X stitch blend**
⊕	453	∫	745/*30745
∕	677	‖	746/*30746
⚡	758	T	783/*33820
✕	945	=	3820/*33820
I	951	◇	3821/*30744
N	3041		**Backstitch**
⊹	3042	∕	154
∷	3045	∕	451
⊠	3740	∕	838
←	3743	∕	930
◸	3770	∕	3045
◱	3823	∕	3064
I	3853	∕	**Gold
♡	3854		**French knots**
⋀	3855	▨	3820

*DMC Rayon thread
**Metallic gold thread

A Stranger Cometh

DMC stranded cotton (floss)

·	Blanc	⊠	646
✚	150	⊟	762
I	211	−	775
■	310	◇	794
✳	318	N	989
◣	319	▽	3064
▣	321	λ	3350
◀	340	✦	3731
<	341	←	3743
▣	367	→	3747
V	402	‖	3752
◤	413	T	3768
◢	414	✖	3772
S	415	△	3816
L	451	✕	*Gold
⊹	452	**Backstitch**	
U	453	◿	Blanc
◆	502	◿	844
↑	504	◹	*Gold
Z	523	**Beads**	
÷	554	●	Turquoise
⁒	562	●	Red

*Metallic gold thread

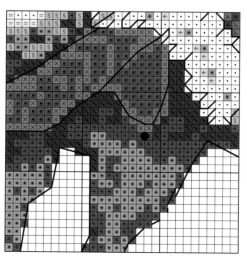

If you are making a gold tassel to attach to the saddle, then use this small section of chart to complete the horse.

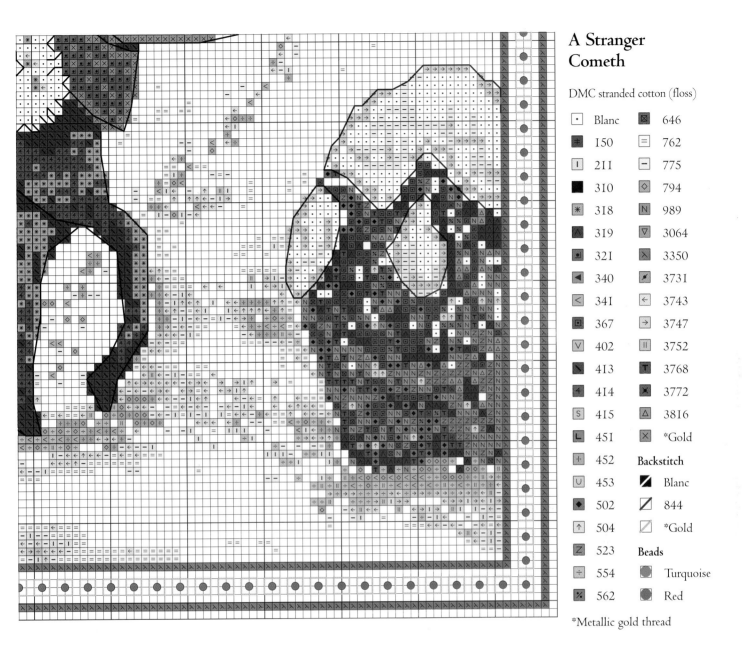

A Stranger Cometh

DMC stranded cotton (floss)

·	Blanc	⊠	646
✚	150	=	762
I	211	−	775
■	310	◇	794
✳	318	N	989
◣	319	▽	3064
▪	321	⊠	3350
◀	340	✗	3731
<	341	←	3743
▣	367	→	3747
V	402	‖	3752
◥	413	T	3768
4	414	✖	3772
S	415	△	3816
L	451	✕	*Gold

⊡	452	**Backstitch**	
U	453	◤	Blanc
◆	502	◢	844
↑	504	◺	*Gold
Z	523	**Beads**	
÷	554	●	Turquoise
%	562	●	Red

*Metallic gold thread

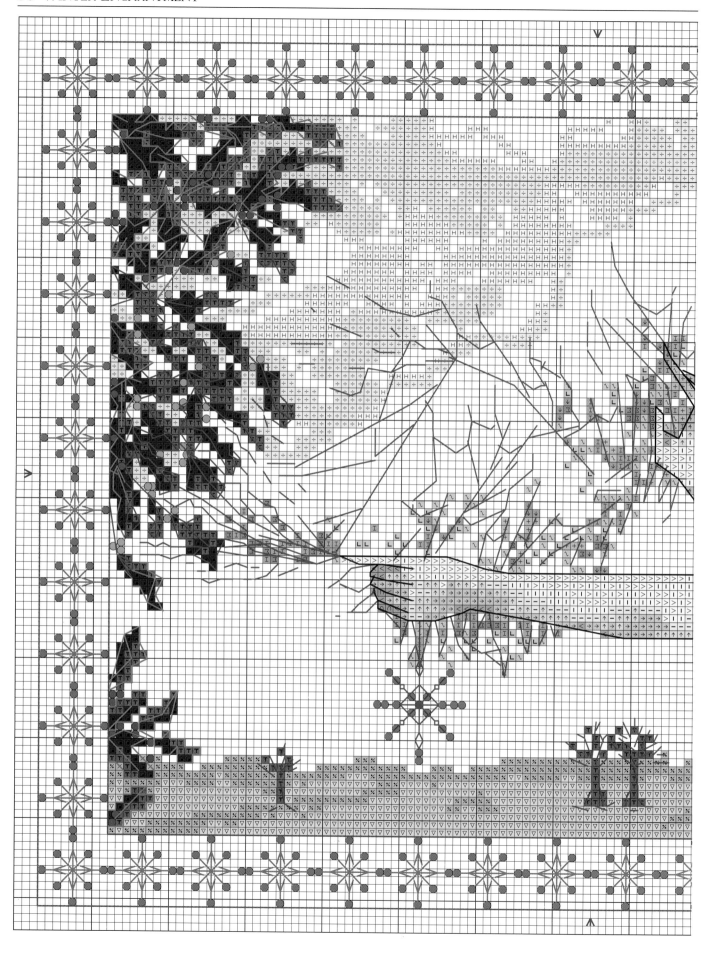

Frost Fairy

DMC stranded cotton (floss)

U	153	÷	775
▽	159	↓	794
⅍	160	⅂	799
<	341	C	800
▥	520	6	3325
T	522	⌄	3747
‖	554	+	3752
–	775	H	3756
∩	794	**Backstitch**	
O	799	╱	Blanc (1)/*White
↑	800	╱	Blanc (2)/*White
✕	3325	╱	161
→	3747	╱	986
4	3752	╱	986 (1)/*White
I	3756	**Beads**	
>	3865	●	Pearl white

½ X stitch

L	159
I	341

● Holly red

● Pink

*Kreinek blending filament

Winter Enchantment Motifs

DMC stranded cotton (floss)

·	Blanc	H	3743
□	223	N	3752
I	225	‖	3753
■	310	I	3756
⌐	340	=	3770
Z	341	S	3807
U	436	O	3813
Λ	502	∩	*Silver
4	648	**Backstitch**	
F	792	⁄	336
L	3042	⁄	*Silver
→	3072	**French knots**	
Σ	3721	⬡	3721

*Metallic silver thread

Oriental Fantasy

*T*he Chinese people have many beliefs that have their roots in folklore and legend, passed down through the generations from father to son and mother to daughter. Over the centuries these legends have evolved and developed: the dragon is one of those stories. Thousands of years ago the first images of the dragon were snake like, but as different clans in ancient China mixed together they realized that the dragon could morph from one form to another. Therefore the Chinese dragon, as we see him today, is a product of imagination; a mythical creature that has evolved into a symbol of harmony and the spirit of the Chinese nation. For most people happiness, prosperity and a long healthy life are the things that they strive for. So by stitching and displaying the Goddess of Mercy, the oriental dragon or the Hok, Lok, Seiw or Sung symbols in a prominent place in your home, you should be blessed with good fortune, health, wealth and harmony

Goddess of Mercy

Legend says that the Chinese Goddess of Mercy was about to enter heaven when the cries of the world reached her ears. Throughout the Orient devotees now seek her guidance. Designed by Saifhon Borisuthibundit

❖ *Blue grey Aida fabric, 14 count 44x38cm (17x15in)*
❖ *DMC stranded cotton (floss) in the colours listed in the key*
❖ *Tapestry needle, No 24*
❖ *Wooden picture frame*

Stitching the Goddess

1 Mark the centre of your Aida fabric with tacking stitches and oversew around the edges to prevent them fraying. Mount the fabric in a frame or embroidery hoop.

2 Work the Goddess from the centre out following the chart and key on pages 48, 49, 50, 51. Use two strands of stranded cotton (floss) for the cross stitch.

3 The backstitch is worked in one strand of stranded cotton (floss). Use black 310 for her eyebrows and eye lashes; 3772 beige for her nose; 351 pink for her mouth; and 839 brown for the markings on her nose, her eye sockets, and under her chin.

4 The backstitch on her hands is done in 839 brown. To give the fingers and arms a rounded appearance each backstitch should be made over several stitches, working around the outline smoothly.

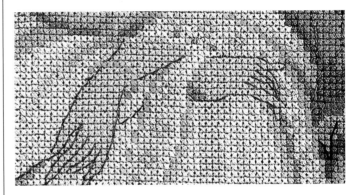

5 Use black 310 for the seed pod, and the veins of the large dark green leaves; 351 pink for the pink flowers; and 839 brown for the markings on the small leaves and the orange flowers.

6 To finish the design, carefully wash and then press the stitching on a soft fluffy towel. Stretch the design following the instructions on page 108, or take the stitching to a framer for stretching and framing.

Oriental Dragon

The dragon stands as the symbol of unity; a mystical creature that has been revered by the Chinese people for centuries, and is the fundamental spirit of Chinese culture.
Designed by Rungrat Puthikul

- *White Aida fabric, 14 count 28x35.5cm (11x14in)*
- *DMC stranded cotton (floss) in the colours listed in the key*
- *Tapestry needle, No 24*
- *White cotton fabric, 30x25.5cm (12x10in) x 2*
- *Wooden dowel – 35.5cm (14in) x 2*
- *Beads – 2.5cm (1in) wooden x 4; 1.5cm (⁵⁄₈in) white x 4; 1cm (³⁄₈in) white x 4*
- *Red tassels x 4*
- *Sewing needle and thread*
- *Orange acrylic paint, paint brush, pen knife, craft glue*

Stitching the dragon

1 Mark the centre of your Aida fabric with tacking stitches and oversew around the edges to prevent them fraying. Mount the fabric in a frame or embroidery hoop.

2 Work the dragon from the centre out following the chart and key on pages 28 and 29. Use two strands of stranded cotton (floss) for the cross stitch and one strand for the backstitch. Wash and press the stitching following the finishing instructions on page 106.

Assembling the wall hanging

1 Turn over the edges of the design on to the wrong side, leaving 2.2cm (⁷⁄₈in) of blank Aida around the stitching. Press the Aida flaps flat against the back of the stitching. Cut a rectangle of white cotton fabric the same size as the stitching. Lay the stitching face down on a flat surface, on top of this place the cotton fabric tucking it under the side and top Aida flaps. Slip stitch the side flaps to the cotton fabric. Fold in the corners at either end of the top flap to form a 'V', and slip stitch the flap to the cotton fabric, but leaving an opening at the sides for the dowel. Repeat with the other flap.

2 Cut a piece of white cotton fabric the same size as the back of the design. Turn in the edges of the cotton fabric so that it just covers the slip stitched Aida edges, but does not cover the gaps left at the corners for the dowel. Slip stitch the cotton fabric on to the back of the stitching.

3 If the dowel is larger than the holes in the beads, you will need to use a pen knife to whittle away some of the wood so that the beads can be pushed on the end. The dowel can be cut with a pen knife, using the same action as sharpening a pencil, but without making a point at the end. Keep trying the beads until you are happy they fit the dowel. Paint the dowel and the wooden beads with several coats of orange acrylic paint.

4 When the paint is completely dry, glue the beads on to one end of the dowel. Slip the tassel in position and thread the dowel into the gap left at the top of the hanging. Slide the second tassel into position and glue the beads on to the other end of the dowel. Repeat for the bottom of the hanging. The dragon can be hung on the wall with a length of plaited red cord looped around the top dowel.

Good Fortune Emblems

These four emblems are believed to bring good fortune to those who own them. Hok symbolizes wealth; Lok is for success; Siew brings a long healthy life; and Sung brings double happiness. Designed by Pinn

❀ *Red Aida fabric, 14 count 15x15cm (6x6in) x 4*

❀ *DMC stranded cotton (floss) in the colours listed in the key*

❀ *Tapestry needle, No 24*

❀ *Red fabric for backing purse*

❀ *Greetings card blank; dressing table mirror*

❀ *Clear plastic coaster – 7.5cm (3in) square*

❀ *Sewing needle and thread*

❀ *Gold cord and button for purse*

Stitching the emblems

1 Mark the centre of your Aida fabric with tacking stitches and oversew around the edges to prevent them fraying. Mount the fabric in an embroidery hoop.

2 Work the emblems from the centre out following the chart and key on the opposite page. Use two strands of stranded cotton (floss) for the cross stitch and one strand for the backstitch. Wash and press the stitching following the finishing instructions on page 108.

Assembling the purse

Cut one piece of stitched Aida, 2cm (¾in) bigger on all sides than the design. Cut the backing fabric to the same size. Place the emblem and the backing fabric right sides together. Stitch around three sides with a 1cm (⅜in) seam allowance. Turn over the top of the purse over on to the wrong side and slip stitch it in place. Turn the purse through to the right side. Sew gold cord down the sides and along the bottom of the purse. Sew a button and loop to the top edge of the purse.

Assembling the mirror and coaster

Use the template provided with the mirror or coaster to cut the fabric to size, then follow the manufacturer's instructions for mounting the stitching.

Making the card

Fray the edges of the stitched emblem before attaching it to the front of a card.

Good Fortune Emblems

DMC stranded cotton (floss)

V	727	4	973
+	922	**Backstitch**	
Σ	971	◿	920
S	972	◿	972

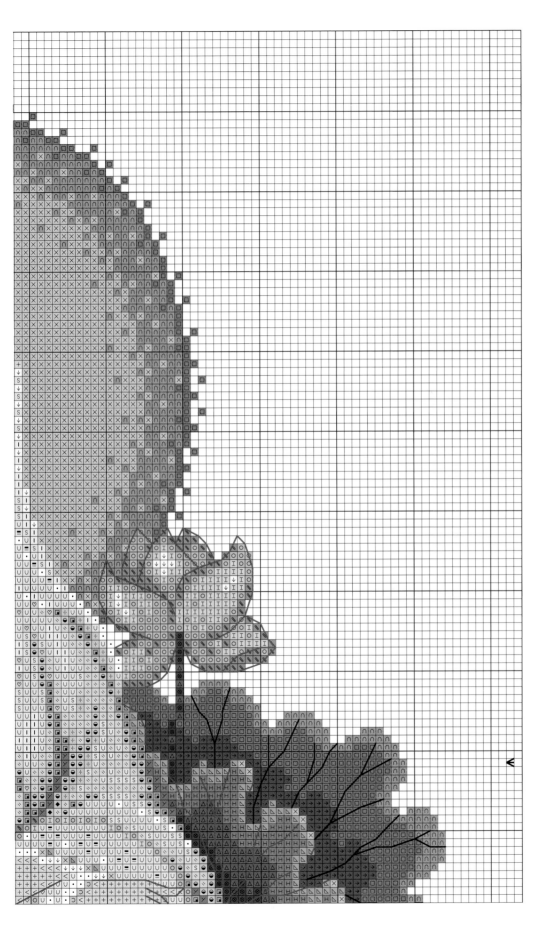

Goddess of Mercy

DMC stranded cotton (floss)

·	Blanc	S	963
U	211	O	972
▲	351	I	973
▢	502	→	986
✛	554	H	3045
⊗	580	∩	3053
△	581	◰	3064
⬈	605	■	3371
✕	676	⋈	3687
✇	721	▣	3688
↓	746	◆	3706
⊃	758	♡	3708
▤	800	↑	3772
I	818	<	3779
▦	839	**Backstitch**	
◖	894	╱	310
▨	938	╱	351
+	945	╱	839
−	951	╱	3772

Goddess of Mercy

DMC stranded cotton (floss)

Symbol	Color	Symbol	Color
·	Blanc	S	963
U	211	O	972
▲	351	I	973
▣	502	→	986
✛	554	H	3045
❀	580	∩	3053
△	581	◣	3064
◸	605	■	3371
✕	676	⋉	3687
✇	721	▣	3688
↓	746	◆	3706
⊃	758	♡	3708
=	800	↑	3772
I	818	<	3779
▰	839	**Backstitch**	
◕	894	╱	310
▣	938	╱	351
+	945	╱	839
−	951	╱	3772

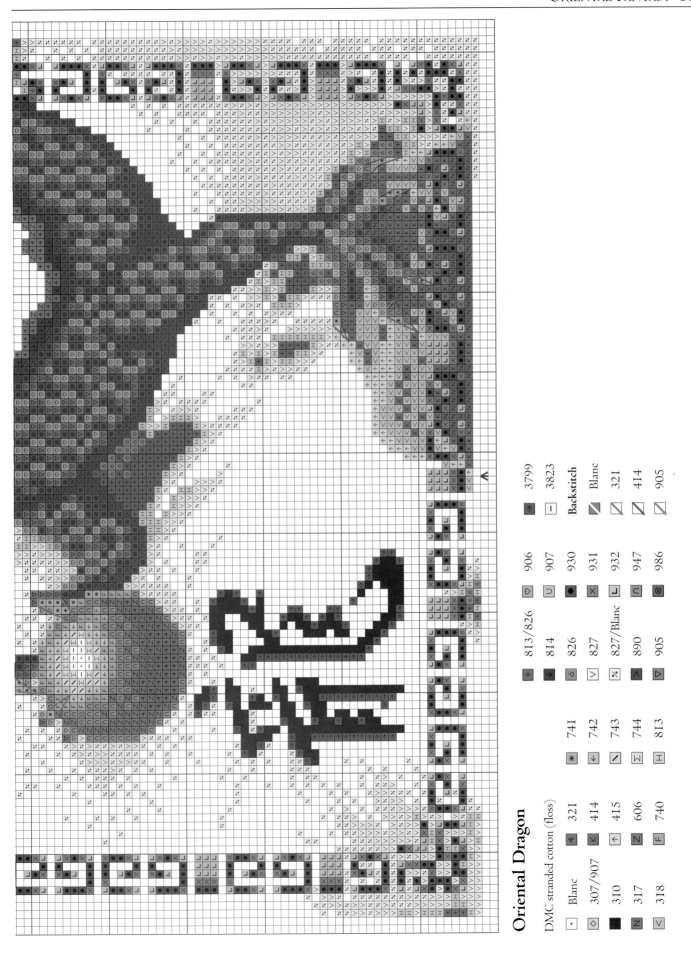

Oriental Dragon

DMC stranded cotton (floss)

·	Blanc	✳	741	+	813/826	↑	3799
◇	307/907	↓	742	➡	814	—	3823
■	310	╱	743	✦	826		**Backstitch**
Ⓝ	317	Σ	744	▽	827	◹	Blanc
V	318	H	813	✕	827/Blanc	◹	321
◀	321			▲	890	◹	414
✕	414			▷	905	◹	905
←	415			◈	906		
N	606			⋃	907		
F	740			●	930		
				✕	931		
				L	932		
				⊂	947		
				⊗	986		

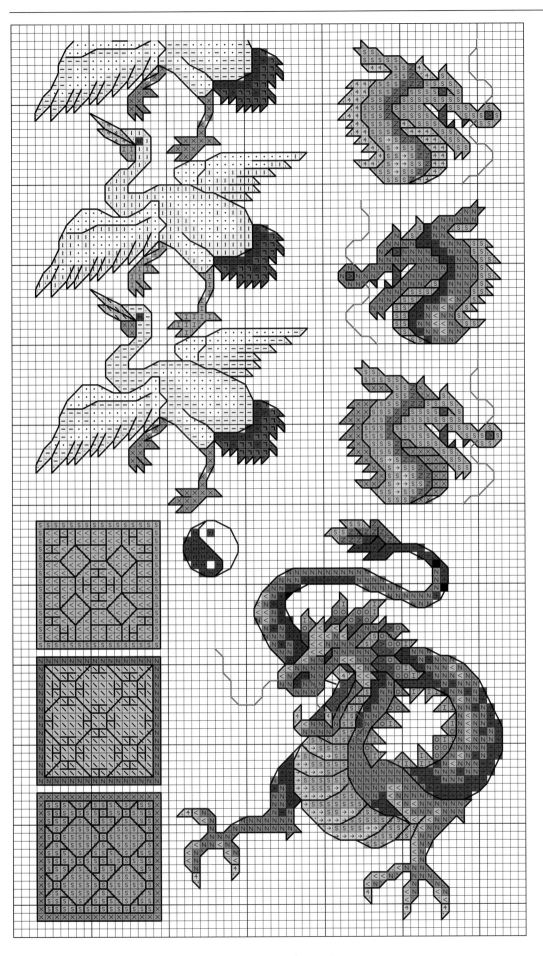

Oriental Fantasy Motifs

DMC stranded cotton (floss)

·	Blanc	−	775
>	349	X	807
O	351	U	842
∩	352	Z	988
⅂	414	S	3348
→	472	T	3765
✓	498	H	3799
◢	561	I	3825
N	562	**Backstitch**	
<	563	╱	349
◥	598	╱	807
4	743	╱	924
I	745	▱	*Gold

*Metallic gold thread

Angelic Messengers

*A*ngelic messengers can take on many guises, and in this chapter you will find three very different examples: a beautiful angel, a cute cherub and the mythical unicorn, all bringing their message of peace and love to the world. Angels are heavenly beings and members of the celestial hierarchy. In mythical art they are mostly portrayed as beautiful women with long hair and wings. The Angel of Peace in this chapter is no exception: a stunning portrait of a woman with shimmering wings and a long flowing gown of turquoise silk. The imaginary unicorn is usually regarded as having the body of a horse. White in colour, the single twisted horn which projects from the middle of its forehead is thought to have magical properties. The unicorn in this chapter can be seen striding through the clouds and early morning mist to greet the newly risen sun. On his back rides a princess, who carries a special message of hope back to her home in the clouds

Angel of Peace

This beautiful angel blows her horn to announce her message of love and peace to the world.
Her flowing gown falls in graceful folds, and her wings shimmer as they catch the sun.
Designed by Mary Stockett

❖ *Antique white evenweave, 27 count 44x35.5cm (17x14in)*
❖ *DMC stranded cotton (floss) in the colours listed in the key*
❖ *Tapestry needle, No 26*
❖ *Kreinek blending filament – pearl, gold*
❖ *Gold frame with decorated mount*

Stitching the angel

1 When choosing fabric for this project, it should be noted that a finer fabric, where the stitches are worked over two strands, should be used. This is because the face is stitched over one thread of fabric. Instructions for working the face are given below. Mark the centre of your evenweave with tacking stitches and oversew around the edges to prevent them fraying. Mount the fabric in a frame.

2 Work the angel from the centre out following the chart and key on pages 64, 65, 66 and 67. Use two strands of stranded cotton (floss) for the cross stitch, apart from the wings which are worked with two strands of stranded cotton (floss) and one strand of pearl blending filament; the yellow dress edge and sleeve linings, are worked using two strands of stranded cotton (floss) and one strand of gold blending filament; and the jewels on the border edge, are stitched in both the light and dark mauve stranded cotton (floss) mixed with a strand of pearl blending filament. So that the blending filament lays flat when stitched, it should be smoothed together with the stranded cotton (floss) before you thread your needle.

3 When working the angel's face each stitch on the chart should be worked over a single fabric thread. This will give the face a finer, detailed appearance. A separate chart for the face can be found on page 67.

Adding the backstitch

1 The backstitch is worked in one strand of stranded cotton (floss). Use grey 414 for the wings; beige 407 for the flesh; charcoal 844 for the eyelashes; brown 433 for the eyebrows; pink 335 for the lips; pink 223 for the ribbon; and beige 782 for the hair and horn. The yellow ribbon at the bottom of the dress and the sleeve linings are backstitched in 3829.

2 The mauve jewels on the border are backstitched in one strand of mauve 327 stranded cotton (floss), mixed with one strand of pearl blending filament.

Mounting and framing

Carefully wash and then press the stitching following the instructions on page 108, or take the stitching to a framer for stretching and framing. Before framing each corner of the fabric can be decorated with a strip of wide lace and a pink ribbon rose.

The Princess and the Unicorn

The mist and clouds swirl around the unicorn as he carries the princess home to her people.
The jewels on the unicorn's breast plate sparkle, touched by the rays of the newly risen sun.
Designed by Susan Penny

❧ *Antique white linen, 32 count 41x30cm (16x12in)*
❧ *DMC stranded cotton (floss) in the colours listed in the key*
❧ *Tapestry needle, No 26*
❧ *DMC gold divisible thread*
❧ *Seed beads — ruby red; Petite beads — pearl, gold*
❧ *Gold horseshoe shaped charm*
❧ *Gold picture frame*

Stitching the design

1 Mark the centre of your linen with tacking stitches and oversew around the edges to prevent them fraying. Mount the fabric in a frame or embroidery hoop.

2 Work the design from the centre out following the chart and key on pages 68 and 69. Use two strands of stranded cotton (floss) for the cross stitch.

3 The clouds can be faded away into the distance by stitching those at the back in half cross stitch using two strands of stranded cotton (floss).

Adding the backstitch

1 The unicorn is backstitched in ecru, and his mouth in brown 3787. The detail around his eye and his horn is also backstitched in brown 3787.

2 The princess's pantaloons are backstitched in mauve 333; her overdress in cerise 915; fur trim in 838; her flesh in 356, and her hair in 632.

3 The crown and detail on the princess's hair, and the decoration on the unicorn's rein is backstitched in one strand of gold metallic thread.

Adding detail to the mane

1 The unicorn's mane and tail can be stitch in backstitch following the chart, or you can use a tufted stitch to give it a three dimensional look. To do this, thread your needle with all six strands of stranded cotton (floss). Starting on the right side of the fabric at the tip of the tail make a stitch into the fabric, bring the needle up a short distance from where you started. Adjust the thread so that one end is the length of the tail hair, then cut the other end to the same length. Continue working up the tail extending the thread towards the middle of the tail, then shortening it a little as you get to the top. Repeat for the mane, then use sharp scissors to shape the tail and mane.

2 Stitch petite gold beads on to the crown, petite pearl beads at the front of the dress, and ruby red seed beads to the unicorn's breast plate. Attach a horseshoe shaped charm to the breast plate, which is marked on the chart with a black dot.

3 Carefully wash, press and then stretch the stitching following the instructions on page 108, or take it to a framer for stretching and framing.

Golden Cherub & Lyre

Throughout the ages, cherubs or winged angels have been used as a symbol of peace. Here we see a golden cherub, and the lyre, both bringing music, love and light to the world.
Designed by Sue Cook

❖ *Cream evenweave, 28 count 18x18cm (7x7in) x 2*
❖ *DMC stranded cotton (floss) in the colours listed in the key*
❖ *Tapestry needle, No 26*
❖ *Ready-made cushion cover approximately 28x28cm (11x11in)*
❖ *Gold ribbon 2cm (³/4in) – approximately 66cm (26in)*
❖ *Gold braid 6mm (¹/4in) – approximately 122cm (48in)*
❖ *Sewing needle and thread*

Stitching the cherub and lyre

Mark the centre point on both pieces of evenweave fabric with a tacking stitch and oversew around the edges to prevent fraying. Stitch the cherub and lyre on to the fabric, using two strands of stranded cotton (floss) for the cross stitch and one for the backstitch, working each stitch over two threads of fabric. Add the beads in the positions marked on the chart with a yellow dot.

Assembling the cushion front

I Place the stitched cherub and lyre on opposite corners of the cushion front. Turn under the two outer edges on both pieces of fabric, so that they fit the cushion front. Pin then tack them in position. Lay a length of gold ribbon horizontally, and then one diagonally on to the cushion front, so that the edges of the stitched fabric are under the ribbon, and the four squares of fabric on the cushion front are equal in size and shape. Machine stitch down the edges on both lengths of ribbon to hold them firmly in place. Slip stitch the turned under edges of the stitched fabric to the side seam of the cushion.

2 Pin then tack a length of gold braid around the edge of the cushion. Slip stitch the braid in position to cover the side seam and the turned under fabric edges.

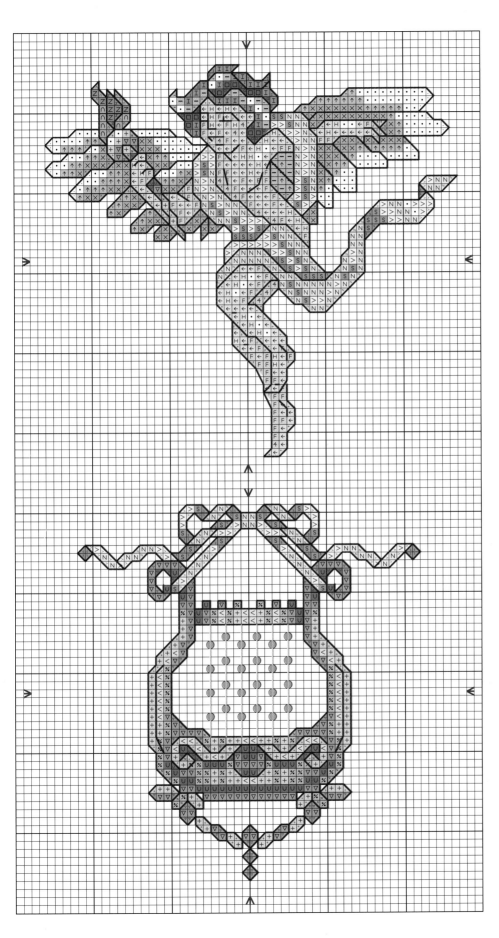

Cherub and Lyre

DMC stranded cotton (floss)

·	Blanc	**Backstitch**	
S	597	⟋	728
✕	644	⟋	838
−	676	**Beads**	
⬓	680	◓	*Gold
⅍	725		
+	727	*V2-08-3820 DMC	
▽	728	Antique Gold seed beads	
I	729		
Z	740		
∩	742		
N	747		
F	754		
≢	780		
U	782		
←	948		
<	3078		
H	3770		
4	3771		
>	3811		
↑	3866		

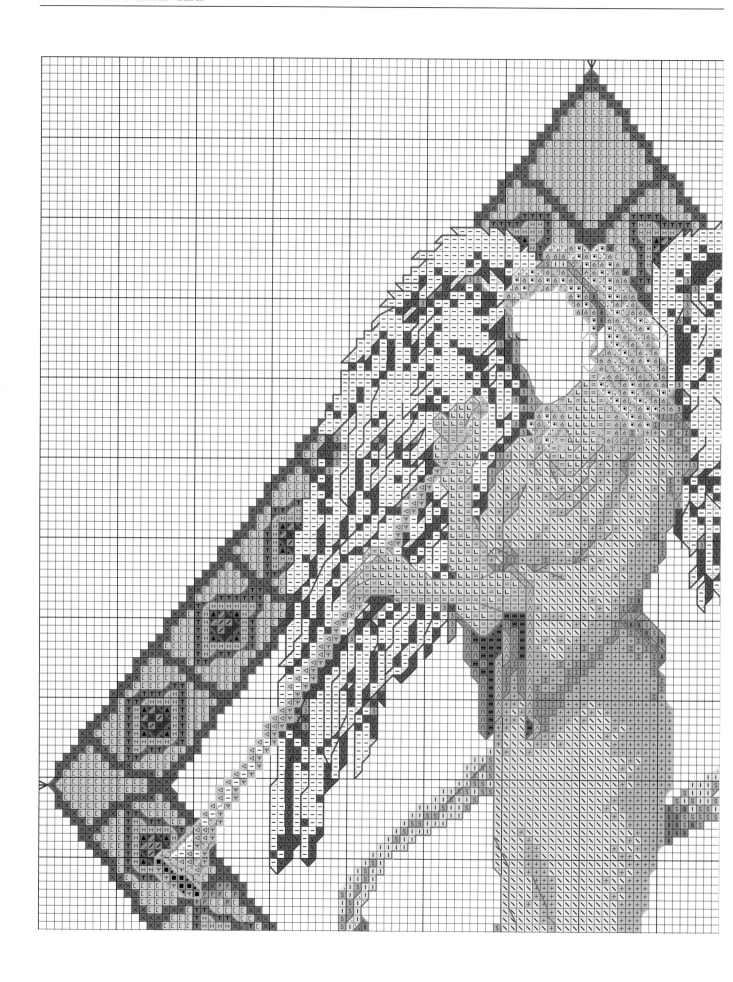

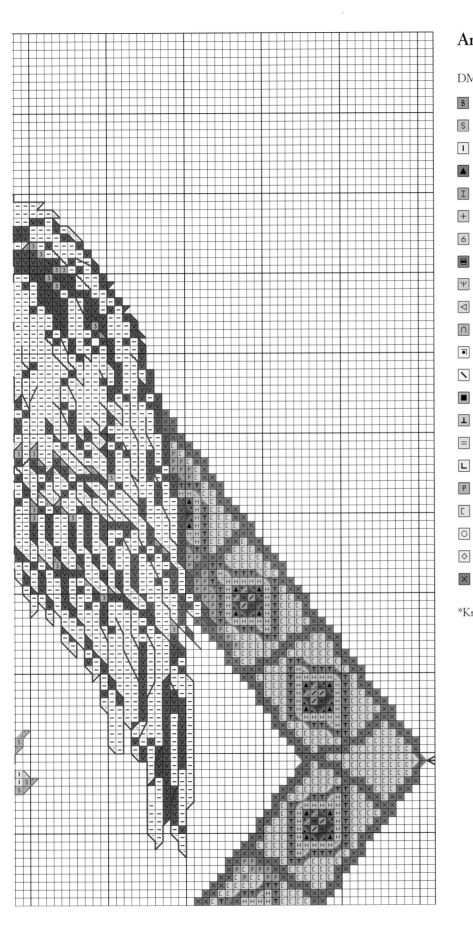

Angel of Peace

DMC stranded cotton (floss)

B	223		**X stitch blend**	
S	224	T	680/3046	
I	225	H	3047/3829	
▲	420		**X stitch blend**	
I	597	–	Blanc/Pearl	
+	598	3	318/*Pearl	
6	676		327/*Pearl	
▣	680	V	415/*Pearl	
Ψ	725	∧	676/*Gold	
◁	726	／	3042/*Pearl	
∩	729		**Backstitch**	
▫	745	╱	223	
＼	747	╱	335	
■	783	╱	407	
⊥	899	╱	414	
=	945	╱	433	
L	951	╱	782	
P	3046	╱	844	
C	3047	╱	3810	
○	3713	╱	3829	
◇	3743		**Backstitch blend**	
X	3829	╱	327/*Pearl	

*Kreinek blending filament

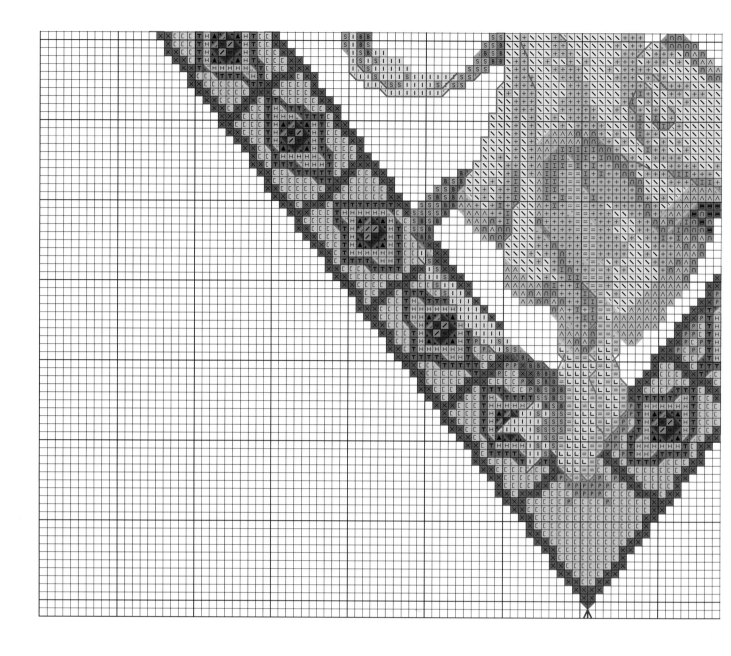

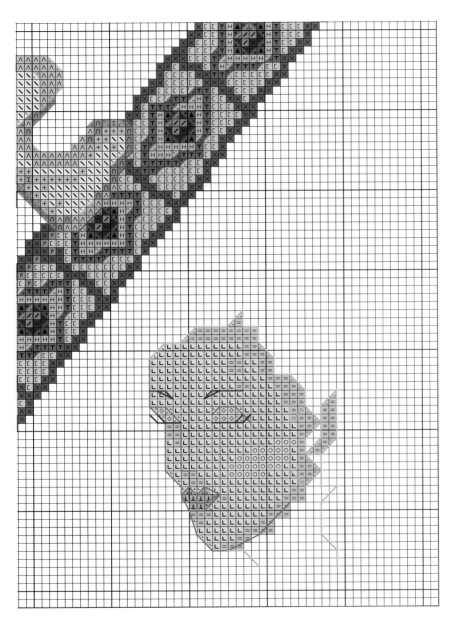

Angel of Peace

DMC stranded cotton (floss)

B	223		X stitch blend
S	224	T	680/3046
I	225	H	3047/3829
▲	420		X stitch blend
I	597	–	Blanc/Pearl
+	598	3	318/*Pearl
6	676	■	327/*Pearl
▣	680	V	415/*Pearl
Ψ	725	∧	676/*Gold
◁	726	/	3042/*Pearl
∩	729		Backstitch
◙	745	/	223
◥	747	/	335
■	783	/	407
⊥	899	/	414
=	945	/	433
L	951	/	782
P	3046	/	844
C	3047	/	3810
O	3713	/	3829
◇	3743		Backstitch blend
✕	3829	/	327/*Pearl

*Kreinek blending filament

Use the small chart above for adding the detail to the face of the angel. Each stitch on the chart should be worked over a single thread of evenweave fabric to give the face a finer, detailed appearance.

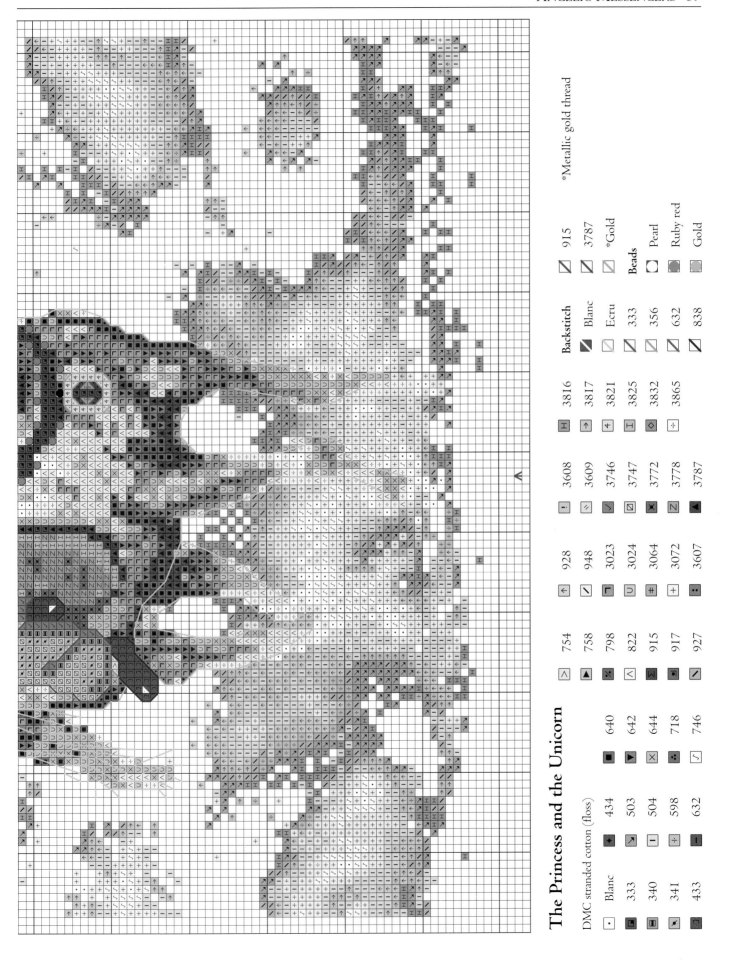

The Princess and the Unicorn

*Metallic gold thread

Angelic Messengers Motifs

DMC stranded cotton (floss)

·	Blanc	O	950
△	368	I	3072
✓	435	→	3753
Z	437	S	3770
❋	646	>	3815
N	648	F	3816
↑	677	H	3864
−	746	X	*Gold
⁒	783	**Backstitch**	
U	818	╱	413
I	827	╱	*Gold
4	828		

*Metallic gold thread

The Mystic Deep

Long ago when explorers travelled the seas under sail, they brought home stories of mystical sea beings, half-human, half-fish that used their magical powers to lure sailors to their death. Some, like the mermaid, were beautiful and beguiling and sang bewitching songs that hypnotized mortals and caused them to drown. Others like Poseidon from Greek mythology, rode his chariot through the waves with unquestionable dominance, and brought fear to anyone who crossed his path. Although the majority of sea tales were tinged with tragedy, those involving dolphins nearly always had a happy ending. Dolphins were once thought to be the saviours of the sea, they were said to rescue drowning sailors from the waves. Today their sense of freedom and fun makes them one of the most loved creatures in the world, and those lucky enough to swim with them find their grace and compassion a spiritual experience. So if you love the sea you are sure to enjoy stitching the projects from The Mystic Deep

Aquamarine

Aquamarine suns herself on the rocks below the walls of the forbidden city. Her long golden hair falls around her shoulders, and her tail glistens and shimmers in the sun.
Designed by Susan Penny from a painting by Linda and Roger Garland

❈ *Cream evenweave, 28 count 46x38cm (18x15in)*
❈ *DMC stranded cotton (floss) in the colours listed in the key*
❈ *DMC rayon in the colours listed in the key*
❈ *Tapestry needle, No 26*
❈ *Seed beads – turquoise and mauve*
❈ *Gold picture frame*

Stitching Aquamarine

1 Mark the centre of your evenweave fabric with tacking stitches and oversew around the edges to prevent them fraying. Mount the fabric in a frame or embroidery hoop.

2 Work Aquamarine from the centre out following the chart and key on pages 80, 81, 82 and 83, and working each stitch over two threads of fabric.

3 Aquamarine's body, face and hair, the sea and the rocks on which she is sitting are worked in cross stitch using two strands of stranded cotton (floss).

4 The forbidden city, cliffs and sky detail are worked in half cross stitch using one strand of stranded cotton (floss).

Working with rayon thread

1 Rayon thread does knot very easily, and so care should be taken to keep the cut lengths and the remainder of the skein organized and together.

2 Use one strand of rayon thread for Aquamarine's tail, the waterfall and porpoise. A few stitches in the water, below the tail and below the waterfall are also worked in rayon thread.

Adding the backstitch

1 The backstitch on the rocks on which Aquamarine is sitting is in one strand rayon thread.

2 The backstitch to outline Aquamarine's body and face is worked in one strand of stranded cotton (floss), but to give the body a rounded appearance each backstitch should be made over several stitches. Work around the outline smoothly, avoiding sharp points and edges.

3 The backstitch on the forbidden city and cliffs should be done as long stitches using one strand of stranded cotton (floss).

4 The backstitch on Aquamarine's tail is also done in longer stitches, but using one strand of rayon thread. Work diamonds for the scales on her tail, and a series of long stitches for the markings on her fin. The shells in her hand and hair, the porpoise and water splashes are also worked as long stitches.

5 The water pouring from the shell is stitched in rayon thread, as a series of overlapping long stitches. This will create the feeling of flowing water.

6 Stitch the mauve beads on Aquamarine's hair, and the turquoise beads at her throat.

Finishing the design

Carefully wash and then press the stitching on a soft fluffy towel. Stretch the design following the instructions on page 108, or take the stitching to a framer for stretching and framing.

Friends from the Deep

❧✿❧

Dolphins have long been linked with sea myths, many of which tell of drowning sailors being rescued by them. In this fantasy globe we can see the magic of these much loved creatures.
Designed by Sue Cook

❀ *Pale blue linen, 28 count 44x44cm (17x17in)*
❀ *DMC stranded cotton (floss) in the colours listed in the key*
❀ *DMC rayon in the colours listed in the key*
❀ *DMC gold metallic thread*
❀ *Kreinek blending filament – 091 yellow, 092 pink*
❀ *Tapestry needle, No 26*
❀ *Seed beads – bright blue, pewter*
❀ *Pearl beads*
❀ *Needle and strong thread*
❀ *Wooden footstool*

Stitching the dolphin globe

1 Mark the centre of your linen with tacking stitches and oversew around the edges to prevent them fraying. Mount the fabric in a frame or embroidery hoop.

2 Work the design from the centre out following the chart and key on page 84 and 85, and working each stitch over two threads of fabric. The general instruction for this design is that the cross stitch and half cross stitch are done in two strands, and the backstitch in one strand. As stranded cotton (floss), rayon thread and Kreinek blending filament are all used in this design, detailed instructions for where to use the threads are given below.

3 All the green and orange cross stitch is worked using two strands of rayon thread, and then backstitched using one strand. Some areas on the oyster shell at the front of the design are also worked in cross stitch using two strands of rayon thread.

4 Some parts of the curly yellow shells are worked using one strand of stranded cotton mixed with one strand of Kreinek blending filament. Lay the two threads together, then thread your needle in the normal way. Blending filament is also used to cross stitch some of the pink areas inside the oyster shell at the front of the design.

5 The half cross stitch around the globe and below the shell at the bottom of the design is done in one strand of stranded cotton. The remainder of the cross stitch is done in two strands of stranded cotton (floss).

6 One strand of gold divisible thread has been used to backstitch the small blue shells, and to add detail to the curly yellow shell either side of the oyster.

7 Stitch a line of pewter beads above each dolphin for bubbles. Use blue beads for the seahorse eyes, and the curly end of the yellow shells either side of the oyster. Stitch two pearl beads in the oyster shell. Carefully wash and then press the stitching on a soft fluffy towel, following the instructions on page 108.

Assembling the footstool

Remove the pad from the footstool. Lay the design centrally over the pad, and then push pins through the fabric into the pad to hold it in position. Thread your sewing needle with a length of strong buttonhole thread. Tie a knot in one end of the thread then begin lacing the stitching across the pad. Work back and forwards in a circle until you reach the point where you started, finish off with a few stitches to hold the lacing securely in place. Remove the pins from the stitching, position the covered pad on the footstool, and tighten the screw on the underside of the base.

Poseidon and his Undersea World

Poseidon, the god of the sea, was said to have spent most of his time in his watery domain.
When he did appear above the waves, he defeated those who crossed his path.
Designed by Maria Diaz

❂ *Pink linen, 28 count 18x20.5cm (7x8in)*
❂ *DMC stranded cotton (floss) in the colours listed in the key*
❂ *DMC silver metallic thread*
❂ *Tapestry needle, No 26*
❂ *Hand towel with inset Aida panel — blue and cream*
❂ *Picture frame decorated with shells*

Stitching Poseidon

1 Mark the centre of your linen with tacking stitches and oversew around the edges to prevent them fraying. Mount the fabric in a frame or embroidery hoop.

2 Work Poseidon from the centre, following the chart on the opposite page. Use two strands of stranded cotton (floss) for the cross stitch and one strand for the backstitch, working each stitch over two threads of fabric.

3 Poseidon's crown, amulets and the end of his trident are worked in one strand of silver metallic thread.

4 Wash and press the stitching following the finishing instructions on page 108. Mount the stitching in a picture frame decorated with sea shells.

Stitching the hand towels

1 Both the hand towels are stitched using two strands of stranded cotton (floss) for the cross stitch, and one strand for the backstitch.

2 Find the centre point of the Aida panel on the towel, and mark it with tacking stitches. Start stitching at this point, repeating the design as many times as is needed to fill the space.

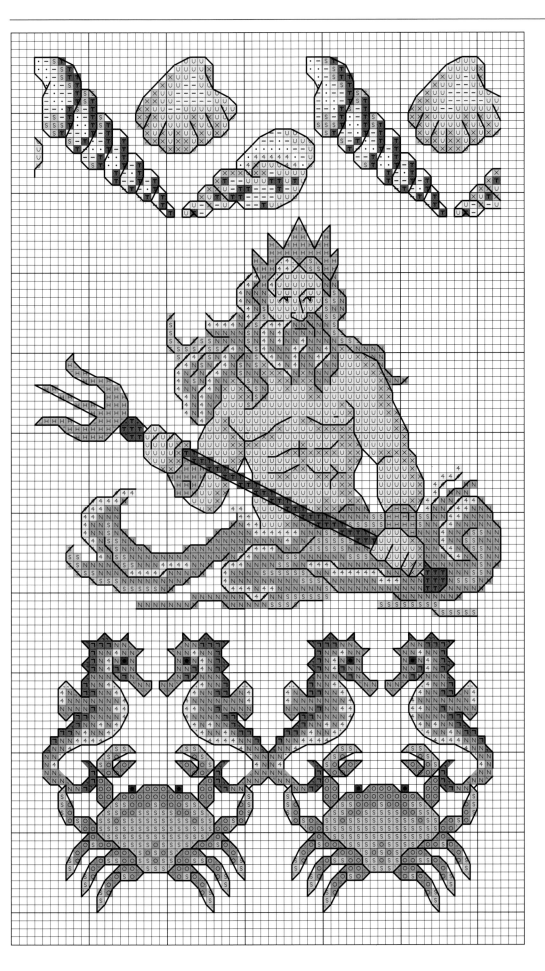

Poseidon and his Undersea World

DMC stranded cotton (floss)

·	Blanc	N	932
O	503	X	950
−	712	U	3770
4	775	T	3772
S	928	H	*Silver
■	930	**Backstitch**	
⌐	931	╱	924

*Metallic silver thread

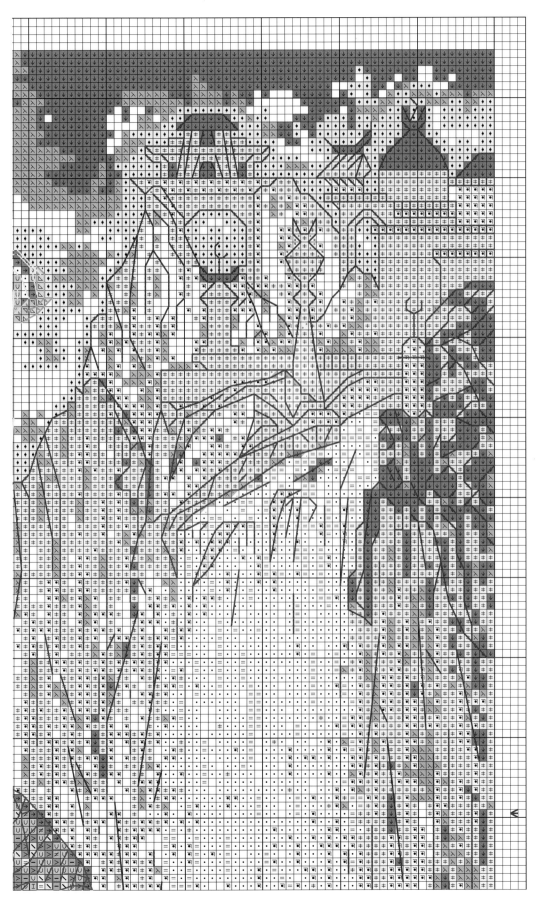

Aquamarine

DMC stranded cotton (floss)

⊙	341	**½ X stitch**	
▣	367	↓	334
▦	501	±	745
✕	502	◆	775
Z	503	⋋	3325
◇	600	▪	3823
◺	758	**Rayon X stitch**	
+	762	⁒	30503
╚	799	→	30553
←	800	U	30554
N	813	=	30762
◹	945	−	30799
6	951	≠	30813
�	3325	╲	30828
<	3340	✕	30943
3	3348	I	30964
∩	3752	>	33814
↑	3773	·	35200
4	3813	**Backstitch**	
✳	3815	╱	334
◉	3816	╱	356
⌀	3817	╱	30798
⌐	3820	☐	30762
S	3821	**Beads**	
‖	3822	●	Mauve
H	3852	◖	Turquoise

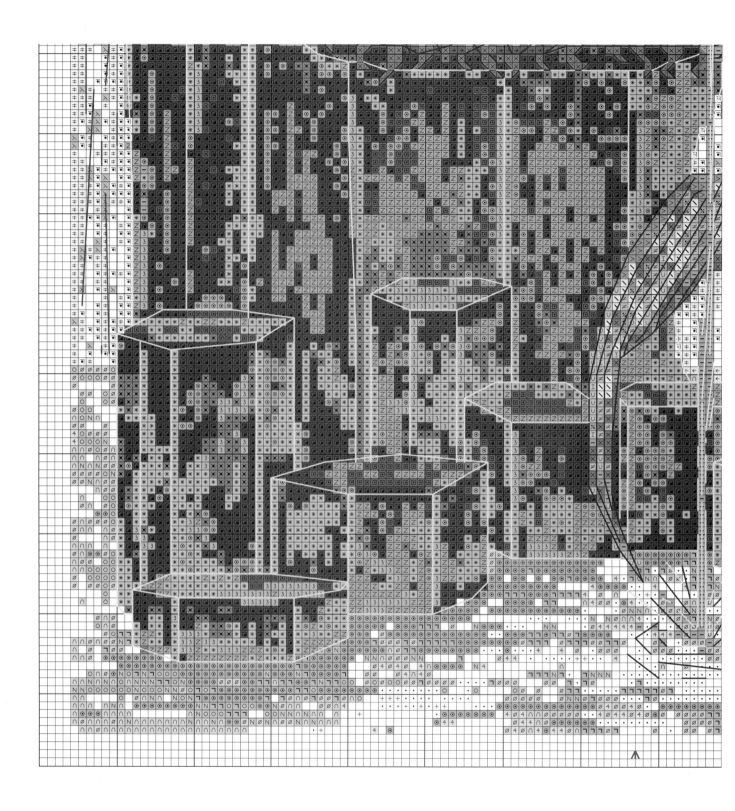

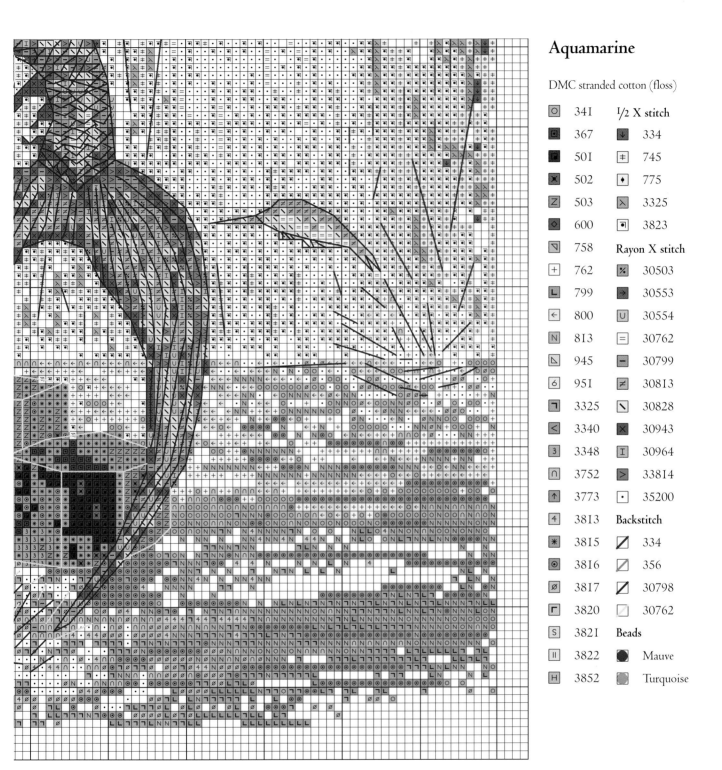

Aquamarine

DMC stranded cotton (floss)

○	341	**¹/₂ X stitch**	
▣	367	↓	334
■	501	±	745
✕	502	◆	775
Z	503	✕	3325
◇	600	▫	3823
◥	758	**Rayon X stitch**	
+	762	⊠	30503
L	799	→	30553
←	800	U	30554
N	813	=	30762
◣	945	−	30799
6	951	≠	30813
⊓	3325	◥	30828
<	3340	✕	30943
3	3348	I	30964
∩	3752	>	33814
↑	3773	·	35200
4	3813	**Backstitch**	
✳	3815	╱	334
⊙	3816	╱	356
∅	3817	╱	30798
⌐	3820	╱	30762
S	3821	**Beads**	
‖	3822	●	Mauve
H	3852	●	Turquoise

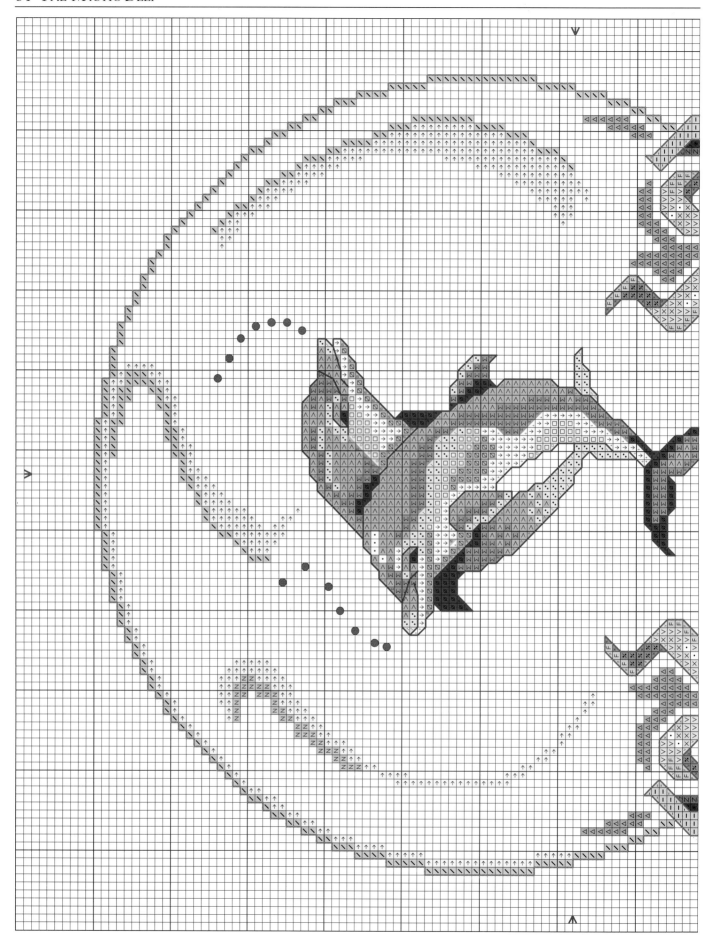

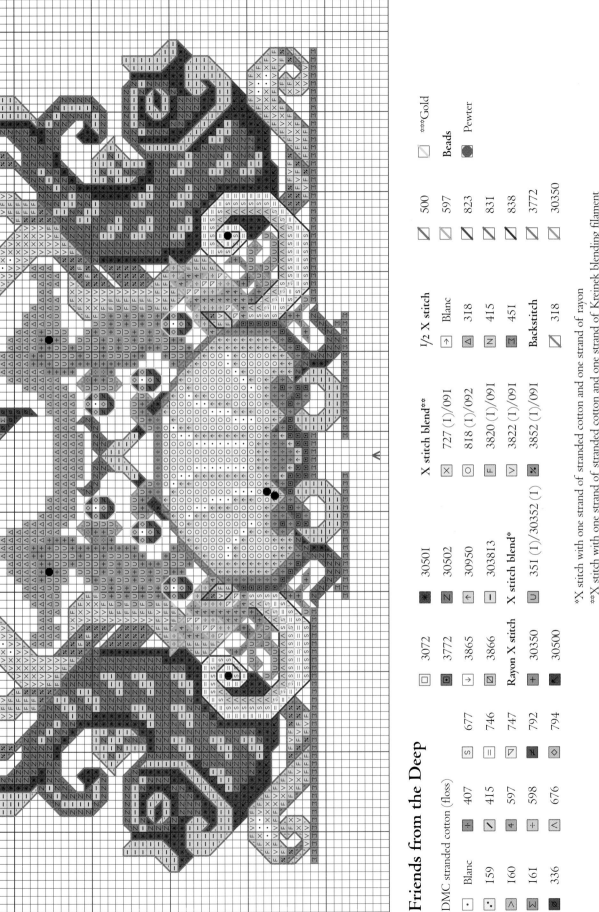

Friends from the Deep

DMC stranded cotton (floss)

·	Blanc			S	677		
·.	159			=	746		
∧	160			▽	747		
Σ	161			⊠	792		
⌀	336			◇	794		
+	407						
⟋	415						
⁴	597						
÷	598						
◁	676						

		X stitch blend**		
▢	3072	✕	727 (1)/091	
⊡	3772	○	818 (1)/092	
→	3865	F	3820 (1)/091	
⊠	3866	▷	3822 (1)/091	
	Rayon X stitch	✻	3852 (1)/091	
U	30350			
+	30500			

		½ X stitch		
✳	30501	↑	Blanc	
N	30502	◁	318	
←	30950	N	415	
—	303813	⋈	451	
	X stitch blend*		Backstitch	
U	351 (1)/30352 (1)	⟋	318	

		Beads	
◹	500		
◹	597		Pewter
◹	823	●	
◹	831		
◹	838		
◹	3772		
◹	30350		

◹	***Gold

*X stitch with one strand of stranded cotton and one strand of rayon
**X stitch with one strand of stranded cotton and one strand of Kreinek blending filament
***Gold metallic thread

Mystic Deep Motifs

DMC stranded cotton (floss)

⊡	Blanc	▽	3341
⊞	518	H	3608
Σ	562	6	3752
O	563	+	3756
>	605	⊡	3768
S	676	N	3770
−	712	∅	3777
I	726	Γ	3778
⊥	729	U	3779
I	762	4	3814
□	793	↓	3830
⅂	926	→	*Silver
⅃	930	↑	**Gold
Z	932	**Backstitch**	
X	950	⁄	924
L	996	⁄	*Silver
=	3078	**French knot**	
T	3340	⬤	209

*Metallic silver thread
**Metallic gold thread

Celestial Heaven

For thousands of years people have used astrology for help and guidance. The study and movements of the celestial bodies was first developed by the Greeks, who used eclipses, comets and the planets to determine war, plague and the weather. Today many people believe that the planets affect our temperament and character, and use astrology as a guide to everyday life. The inspiration for the wallhanging in this chapter is taken from Greek architecture. Cypress trees and classical urns rise up from the bottom, whilst the centre panel is designed as an old manuscript on which sit the twelve signs of the zodiac. At the top a Greek god, surrounded by the night sky, holds the world under his arm, whilst he leans on a panel containing an image of the sun and moon. Celestial Heaven offers endless possibilities for stitching, and whether you take these ancient beliefs seriously or not, any part of this wonderful design is a work of art in its own right

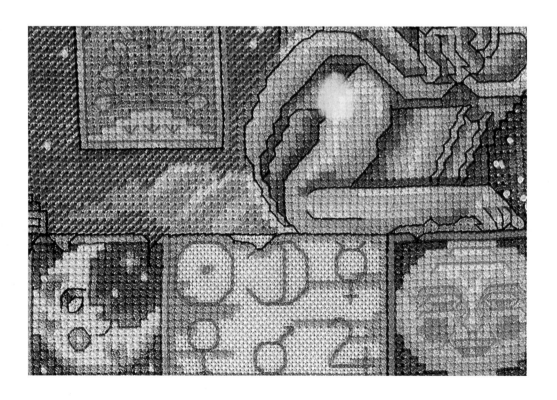

Celestial Heaven

❧❀❧

Shades of violet, blue and gold have been used to create this stunning astrological design.
The twelve zodiac signs in the middle can each be stitched into a card or keepsake.
Designed by Sue Cook

❀ *White evenweave fabric, 28 count 70x53.5cm (28x21in)*

❀ *White evenweave fabric, 28 count 12x12cm (4³/₄x4³/₄in)*
for each zodiac motif

❀ *DMC stranded cotton (floss) in the colours listed in the key*

❀ *Tapestry needle, No 26*

❀ *Iron-on vilene 70x53.5cm (28x21in)*

❀ *Burgundy velvet – 12x66.6cm (4³/₄ x 26¹/₄in) x 2;*
78x14.5 (30³/₄x5³/₄in) x 2; 78x66.6cm
(30³/₄x26¹/₄in) x 1

❀ *Sewing needle and thread*

❀ *Clear plastic coaster 8x8cm (3¹/₈x3¹/₈in)*

❀ *Greetings card blanks*

❀ *Scraps of sheer fabric and cord to decorate the cards*

❀ *Stiff cardboard 16x8cm (6¹/₂x3¹/₈in)*

❀ *Pole for displaying wallhanging*

❀ *Upholstery cord, tassel*

❀ *Scissors, double-sided tape, compass, pencil*

Stitching the wallhanging

1 Mark the centre of your evenweave with tacking stitches and oversew around the edges to prevent them fraying. Mount the fabric in a frame.

2 Work the design from the centre out following the chart and key on pages 94 – 103. As the design is split over ten pages, a diagram is shown several times on the chart pages to help you with the position of each section.

3 Use two strands of stranded cotton (floss) for the cross stitch and half cross stitch. The half cross stitch is used for the sea and sky area in the landscape at the bottom of the design; the blue sky up the sides; and the blue sky at the top between the pillars. Several smaller areas

of stitching are also done in half cross stitch, these can be identified using the key.

4 All the french knots and backstitch are done in one strand of stranded cotton (floss). Use 838 for the buildings, zodiac signs, outer manuscript and border line; 782 yellow for the patterns between the signs, and pictorial rectangles between pillars; 580 green for the trees; 740 orange for the moon; and 333 blue for the moons below the pillars at the top of the design.

Assembling the wall hanging

1 Wash and press the stitching. Place a blanket or large towel on a flat surface, on top of this place the stitching face down. Lay the vilene on top, and using a hot iron, without steam, iron the vilene on to the back of the stitching. Trim the stitching leaving 5cm (2in) on all edges. Following the measurements on the left, cut two identical velvet strips, one for each side of the wallhanging; one strip for the top and bottom of the wallhanging; and a rectangle for the back.

2 Pin the velvet strips around the edges of the stitching, right sides together, leaving 1cm (³/₈in) of blank evenweave between the design and the velvet border edge. Sew the top and bottom strips on to the stitching with a 1cm (³/₈in) seam allowance. Next, sew on the side strips, extending the stitching over the top and bottom velvet strips.

3 Place the assembled front and the backing velvet right-sides together. With a 1cm (³/₈in) seam allowance sew the back and front together, leaving the top edge open. Turn the wallhanging through to the right side. Gently press the seams with a warm iron, making sure you cover them with a soft cloth to prevent the pile flattening.

4 Cut several lengths of burgundy ribbon. Fold each piece of ribbon in half, and then place the cut ends in the opening at the top of the wallhanging, using a tape measure to space them equally across the top. Pin and then tack the ribbon hangers in position.

5 Sew the ribbon firmly to the seam allowance, then slip stitch the top of the wallhanging closed. A pole can now be inserted through the hangers. Alternatively, sew a strip of velvet fabric, horizontally, on to the back of the wallhanging to take the pole.

Stitching the zodiac signs

1 Mark the centre of your evenweave with tacking stitches and oversew around the edges to prevent them fraying. Mount the fabric in a hoop.

2 Work the zodiac sign from the centre out following the chart and key on pages 94 – 103. Use two strands of stranded cotton (floss) for the cross stitch, and one strand for the backstitch.

3 Wash and press your stitching following the instructions on page 108.

Assembling the zodiac signs

1 Using the template on page 104, cut two 8cm (3⅛in) circle from cardboard. Cut your stitched fabric into a circle leaving enough fabric to wrap around the cardboard circle.

2 Stick double-sided tape on to both sides of the cardboard circle. Lay the stitched design on to the tape, and making sure the design is in the centre, press the fabric well down to hold it in place. Turn the cardboard over, and ease the excess fabric at the back on to the double-sided tape. Secure the excess fabric at the back with a few lacing stitches to hold it firmly in place.

3 If you are making a hanging or mobile you will need to make a second fabric covered circle to cover the back of the stitching. You can either use blank evenweave fabric; a coloured fabric like velvet; or you may prefer to stitch another zodiac sign.

Assembling the zodiac mobile

1 Place two fabric covered circles together. If you are using two stitched designs you will need to twist one to make sure they are both the same way up. Pin the circles together, then slip stitch using small neat stitches.

2 Cut a length of cord to fit around the circle. Push one cord end between the stitches that hold the cardboard circles together. Pin the cord around the edge, to cover the seam where the two cardboard circles meet. Tuck the other end of the cord in next to the first, and slip stitch the cord in place.

3 The completed roundel can now be attached to a length of upholstery cord. Stitch a tassel to the bottom of the roundel, and then decorate the cord with star shaped beads.

Assembling the card

1 Attach the stitched zodiac sign to a cardboard circle following the instructions 1 & 2 for assembling the zodiac signs. Do not make a second covered circle to cover the back.

2 Decorate the front of a blank greetings card with sheer fabric and cord, then attach the roundel with double-sided tape.

Assembling the coaster

1 Lay vilene on top of the stitched design, and using a hot iron, without steam, iron the vilene on to the back – this will stop the fabric fraying.

2 Using the template provided with the coaster, cut the stitched design to the correct size. Place the design inside the coaster and snap on the back.

Celestial Heaven

DMC stranded cotton (floss)

•	Blanc	**½ X stitch**	
▽	165	↘	155
ø	166	⁚	224
/	168	//	225
F	169	⊙	333
○	333	3	340
S	340	‡	341
•	341	∧	519
T	580	‖	742
Z	581	∩	3041
×	642	⊥	3042
⋱	644	4	3078
–	645	H	3746
↓	677	√	3747
←	726	⊡	3760
✳	728	⋋	3761
÷	740	**Backstitch**	
♡	742	/	333
=	744	/	580
✢	780	/	645
↖	782	/	740
╲	822	/	782
◺	3022	/	838
N	3023	**French knots**	
I	3041	○	Blanc
I	3078		
□	3746		
✓	3747		

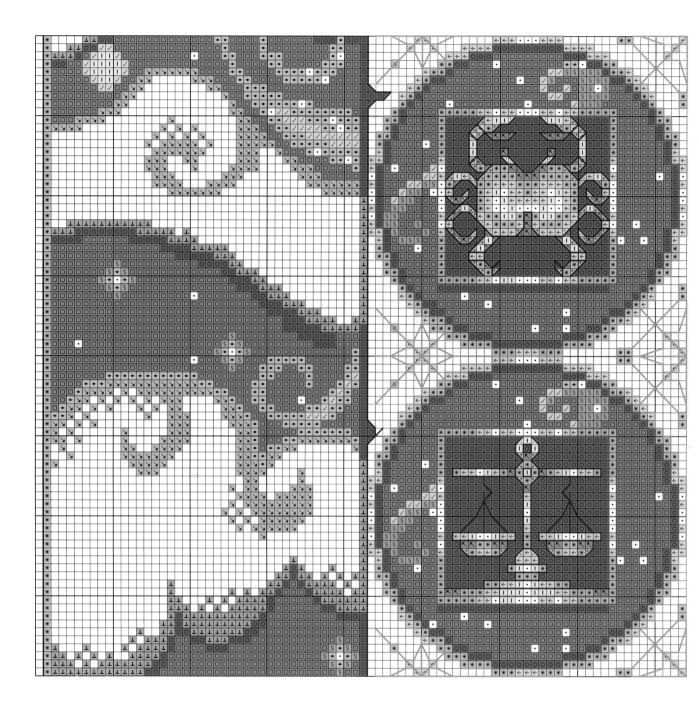

Celestial Heaven

DMC stranded cotton (floss)

·	Blanc	**¹/₂ X stitch**	
▽	165	◣	155
ø	166	⦂	224
╱	168	⁄	225
F	169	⊙	333
O	333	3	340
S	340	∓	341
◆	341	∧	519
▦	580	‖	742
◪	581	∩	3041
X	642	⊥	3042
◥	644	4	3078
▓	645	H	3746
↓	677	∫	3747
←	726	▣	3760
✳	728	╲	3761
∔	740	**Backstitch**	
♡	742	╱	333
=	744	╱	580
✚	780	╱	645
◤	782	╱	740
◥	822	╱	782
◣	3022	╱	838
N	3023	**French knots**	
I	3041	◯	Blanc
I	3078		
▢	3746		
✓	3747		

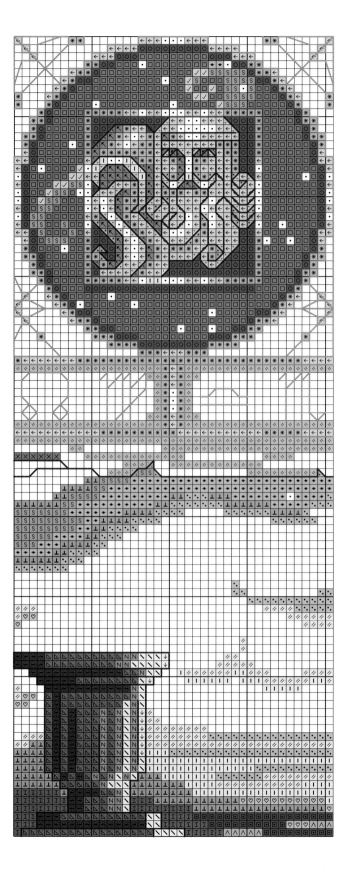

Celestial Heaven

DMC stranded cotton (floss)

·	Blanc	½ X stitch	
▽	165	↘	155
ø	166	∴	224
✓	168	⧄	225
F	169	⊙	333
O	333	3	340
S	340	±	341
•	341	∧	519
▼	580	‖	742
Z	581	∩	3041
X	642	⊥	3042
↘	644	4	3078
■	645	⊞	3746
↓	677	∫	3747
←	726	⊡	3760
✳	728	⋋	3761
÷	740	**Backstitch**	
♡	742	⧄	333
=	744	⧄	580
✚	780	⧄	645
◤	782	⧄	740
↘	822	⧄	782
◣	3022	⧄	838
N	3023	**French knots**	
I	3041	◯	Blanc
I	3078		
▢	3746		
✓	3747		

Celestial Heaven

DMC stranded cotton (floss)

·	Blanc	◆	341	←	726	◣	822	½ X stitch		∧	519	▣	3760	▱ 782
▽	165	☈	580	✳	728	◣	3022	↘	155	‖	742	⊠	3761	▱ 838
⌀	166	▨	581	÷	740	N	3023	⦂	224	⌒	3041	Backstitch		French knots
◿	168	✕	642	♡	742	⫿	3041	⫽	225	⊥	3042	▱	333	◯ Blanc
F	169	◥	644	=	744	∣	3078	⊙	333	4	3078	▱	580	
◉	333	▦	645	⊕	780	▢	3746	3	340	H	3746	▱	645	
S	340	↓	677	◤	782	✓	3747	‡	341	◿	3747	▱	740	

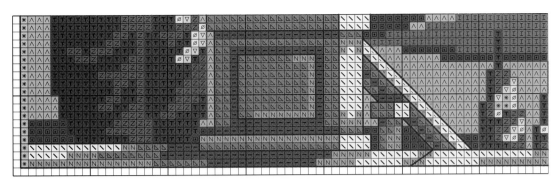

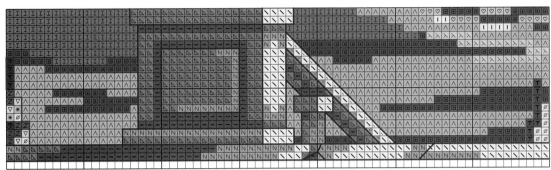

These three sections form the lower part of the chart. The plan below shows how the chart is split; the numbers refer to the page on which the chart section can be found.

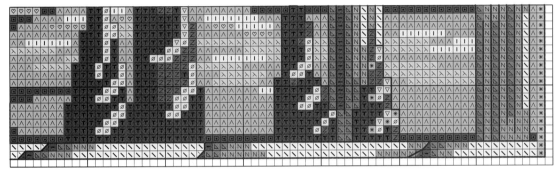

Celestial Heaven

DMC stranded cotton (floss)

·	Blanc	↘	644	∟	3022	3	340	**Backstitch**
▽	165	▦	645	N	3023	±	341	╱ 333
∅	166	↓	677	I	3041	∧	519	╱ 580
╱	168	←	726	∣	3078	‖	742	╱ 645
F	169	✳	728	□	3746	∩	3041	╱ 740
O	333	÷	740	✓	3747	⊥	3042	╱ 782
S	340	♡	742	**1/2 X stitch**		4	3078	╱ 838
•	341	=	744	↘	155	H	3746	**French knots**
T	580	⊹	780	·.	224	✓	3747	◔ Blanc
Z	581	◤	782	⁄⁄	225	▦	3760	
X	642	↖	822	⊙	333	↘	3761	

Use the templates on this page to make the Merlin wallhanging and zodiac mobile.

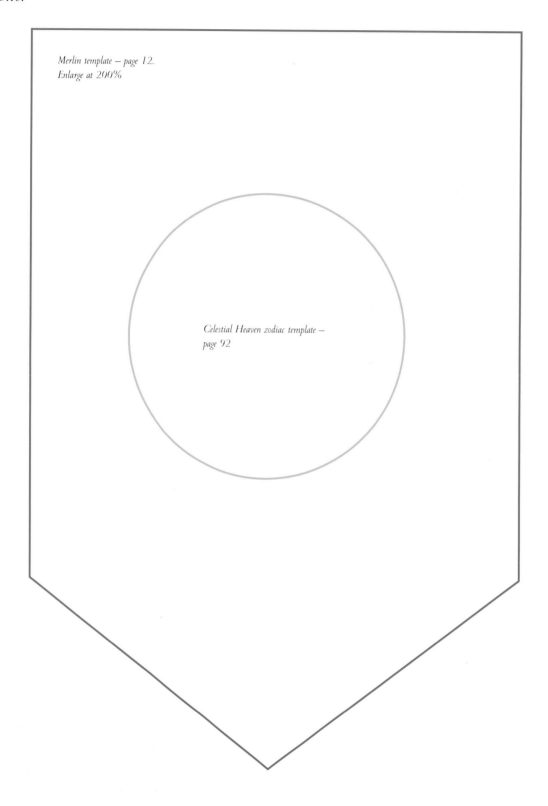

Merlin template — page 12.
Enlarge at 200%

Celestial Heaven zodiac template —
page 92

Stitching Techniques

Most of the designs in this book are simple to stitch — a combination of cross stitch and backstitch, with detail added using half cross stitch, french knots and beads. Below you will find working instructions for the stitches, and useful information on reading the charts

General stitching instructions

On projects where a fine evenweave fabric is used, each stitch should be worked over two threads of the fabric; where Aida fabric is used each stitch should be worked over one block of fabric. The number of strands of stranded cotton (floss) for each stitch will be listed in the instructions for that project. The stitches used in this book are: cross stitch, three-quarter stitch, half cross stitch, backstitch and French knots; beads and specialist threads are used on some projects. On the princess and the dragon (page 11), some stitches are worked with two different colours of stranded cotton (floss) in the needle, this is called blended needle or tweeding (more details see page 106). On the angel of peace (page 59), one strand of blending filament is added to the needle with the stranded cotton (floss) to make the thread shine. Where rayon thread is used in a project, stranded cotton (floss) can be used in its place, as the colours numbers are the same as the stranded cotton colours.

Understanding the charts

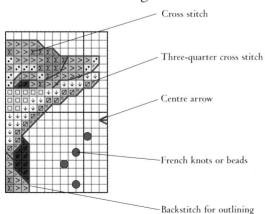

Cross stitch

Three-quarter cross stitch

Centre arrow

French knots or beads

Backstitch for outlining

A section of chart showing some of the stitches used on the designs in this book: cross stitch, three-quarter stitch, backstitch, french knots and beads.

Reading the charts

The charts are in colour, with a symbol printed in each square. Each square on the chart represents one cross stitch. In some cases, on finer fabric, each square on the chart is worked over two threads of fabric. All the charts have a key listing the DMC stranded cotton (floss) colours used in number order. The key also shows if there is backstitch, french knots and beads, and whether blending filament or blended needle has been used for that stitch (see 106). The french knots and beads are shown as coloured dots on the key and chart (more details on beads can be found in working with beads on the next page). If you would prefer not to use beads then french knots can be used in their place. Most designs have a combination of whole cross stitch, three-quarter stitch and backstitch, a few designs use half cross stitch. The three-quarter stitches are shown on the chart as triangles of colour printed in the corners of a square; each half cross stitch appears on the chart in the same way as a full cross stitch, but in the key is listed separately below the cross stitch. As well as a chart and key, each design has a list of materials and working instructions.

Fabric

The designs in this book are worked on Aida or evenweave fabric like linen. All the fabrics used for cross stitch should have the same number of horizontal and vertical threads to the inch. Aida has threads grouped together in blocks, so that one stitch is made over one block of threads using the holes as a guide. When working on the finer evenweave, like 36 count, the instructions may tell you to make each stitch over one, two or even four threads of fabric. On the angel of peace (page 59) the face is worked over one thread, while the rest of the design is worked over two: this gives the features a realistic appearance. A project sewn over two threads on 28 count fabric, for example, would come out the same size as if you stitched it on 14 count Aida. The fabric listed in the key shows the count, the colour, and the size of fabric needed for the design. When buying the fabric allow extra at the edges if you are intending to work the design in a hoop or small frame. If you want to stitch on a different count of fabric than shown on the project, you will have to calculate the finished size of the stitching before you buy the fabric. To do this, count the number of squares both high and wide of your chosen design – this is the stitch count. Then divide the two measurements by the number of threads per inch of your fabric. When you are stitching over two threads remember to divide the stitch count by half the number of threads per inch.

Needle and thread

Use a needle for cross stitch that is blunt and slips easily through the fabric without piercing it. A size 24 tapestry needle works best on 14 count Aida, while a 26 tapestry needle is best for finer fabric. A 26 tapestry needle should easily pass through the eye of most beads, but you may find that using a fine sewing needle is easier on some designs. The designs are stitched using DMC stranded cotton, DMC rayon thread, DMC divisible metallic and Kreinek blending filament; the number of strands needed for each stitch is in the project instructions.

Using blending filament

Blending filament can be mixed with stranded cotton (floss) to give the stitches a shiny appearance. Cut a length of filament the same size as the stranded cotton (floss). So that the threads stay flat when stitched, they should be smoothed together before threading your needle. A single strand of blending filament should be enough to give the stranded cotton (floss) a shiny appearance.

Using rayon thread

Rayon thread is very slippery and can be difficult to work with unless handled properly. Once you have cut a length from the skein make sure it is laid flat on your working surface, or it may become tangled. Carefully separate the threads from the length, and then recombine the number you need to stitch with before threading your needle. It may make the rayon thread easier to work with if you use a strand of stranded cotton (floss) in the needle as well as the rayon.

Blended needle

On some designs blended needle has been used to give the stitches a tweeded appearance. If a symbol in the key has two colour numbers listed against it you will need to thread your needle with one strand of each colour. So on page 16, where colour 522 and colour 523 are listed against one symbol, take one strand of each colour, lay them together and then thread your needle. Each stitch will then have a tweeded appearance.

Working with beads

The beads are shown on the charts and keys as coloured dots. For more details on understanding the charts and keys see reading the charts, at the beginning of this chapter. Most of the beads used in this book match DMC stranded cotton (floss) colours. There are four different type of DMC beads: V1 general seed beads, V2 nostalgia, V3 metallic and V4 frosted. As well as the bead type, a colour code and colour description will also be listed. The beads should be attached to the stitching using two strands of stranded cotton (floss). Thread the bead on to the needle as you make the first part of the cross, then as you make the second part, lay one thread of stranded cotton (floss) either side of the bead, before pushing the needle back into the fabric and continuing.

Working the stitches

Cross stitch Each coloured square on the chart represents one cross stitch on the fabric. A cross stitch is worked in two stages: a diagonal stitch is worked over one block of Aida, or two threads of finer evenweave fabric like linen, from the bottom left of the stitch to the top right. The second part of the stitch is worked from bottom right to top left to form a cross. When working a block of stitches in the same colour, stitch a line of half crosses before completing each stitch on the return journey. Make sure that the top half of each cross lies in the same direction.

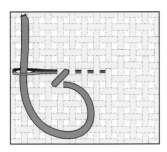

Half cross stitch The stitches are shown on the chart as full symbols in the same way as cross stitch, but on the key they are listed in a separate section. A half cross stitch is just the first part of a full cross stitch: a diagonal stitch worked over one block of Aida, or two threads of linen from the bottom left to the top right. Half cross stitch works well in areas of the stitching where you want a less solid effect.

Three-quarter stitch Each stitch is shown on the chart as a coloured triangle. A three-quarter stitch is a half stitch (the first part of a cross stitch) with a quarter stitch worked from one of the remaining corners to the middle of the stitch. It is easier to work fractional stitches when each stitch is being worked over two threads of fabric (like linen or fine evenweave). When stitching on Aida you will have to pierce the middle of the fabric block with a sharp needle to make a hole for the quarter stitch.

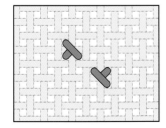

Backstitch This is shown on the chart as a solid coloured line, and may be used on the chart in several different ways: as an outline to give definition to an area of stitches; on top of the cross stitch to give detail; on its own, to create areas of lettering or detail lines. Backstitch can be worked as single stitches over one or two threads of fabric, or as longer stitches to cover a larger area.

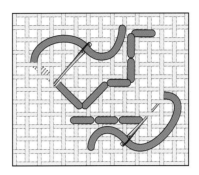

Preparing to stitch

Cut your fabric several inches larger than the size given in the project materials list. Zig-zag around the edges of the fabric or bind it with masking tape to prevent the edges fraying. Fold the fabric in four to find the centre point, and mark it with a pin or small stitch. Find the centre of the chart by following the arrows from the edges to the centre – this is where you begin stitching. Thread your needle and make a knot at one end of the thread. Push the needle to the back of the fabric about 3cm (1¼in) from your starting point, leaving the knot on the right side. Stitch towards the knot, securing

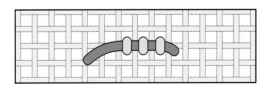

the thread on the back of the fabric. When the thread is secure, cut off the knot. When you have finished stitching, finish the thread by weaving it through the back of the stitches.

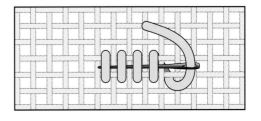

Hoop or frame

Larger projects will need to be supported in a hoop or on a frame whilst you are stitching. Before cutting your fabric check carefully how much you will need, allowing extra for lacing it to a frame. If you are using a hoop you will still need to add extra fabric around the design to hold it in the hoop. Always remove the project from the hoop when you are not working to prevent a ring mark forming on the fabric. Once the stitching has been completed the excess fabric can be cut away.

Washing and pressing

Handling even the smallest piece of cross stitch can make the threads look flat and dull, so always wash your work before it is framed or mounted. To do this, swish the stitching in luke warm water and, if the colours bleed, rinse in fresh water until the water is clear. Do not be tempted to stop rinsing unless you are absolutely sure the bleeding has stopped. Roll the stitching in a clean towel and squeeze gently to remove most of the water. On a second fluffy towel, place your design face down, cover with a clean cloth and iron until the stitching is dry.

Mounting and framing

It is best to take large cross stitch designs to a professional framer who will advise you on displaying your work. If you would prefer to lace your own work then most framers will be happy to make the frame and cut the mount and backboard for you. If you are mounting the work yourself use acid-free board in a pale colour. The mount board should be cut to fit inside your picture frame, allowing for the thickness of material that will be wrapped over the board. There are two methods of attaching the stitching to the board – taping and lacing.

Taping

Place the cut board on the reverse side of your stitching. Starting from the centre of one of the longest sides, fold the excess fabric over on to the board, then pin through the fabric and into the edge of the board.

Repeat along all four sides of the board. Use strips of double-sided tape to hold the fabric on to the back of the board. Remove the pins once the work is secured.

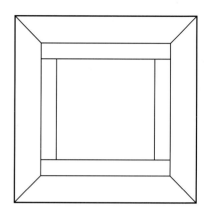

Lacing

Pin the work along the edges of the board in the same way as for the taping. Working from the centre of one side, and using very long lengths of strong thread begin lacing backwards and forwards across the gap between the fabric overlap, while keeping the fabric on the right side stretched. Remove the pins. Repeat for the other two sides, taking care to mitre the corners or turn the corners in neatly.

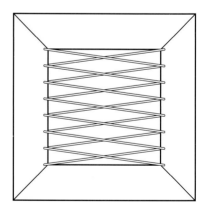

Suppliers

When writing to any of the companies below, please include a stamped addressed envelope for your reply.

DMC Creative World Ltd
Pullman Road, Wigston, Leicester LE8 2DY
Aida, linen, stranded cotton, metallic divisible thread, rayon thread and beads.

Coats Crafts Ltd
PO Box 22, The Lingfield Estate, McMullen Road,
Darlington, Co Durham DL1 1YQ
Kreinek blending filament.

Craft Creations Ltd
2C Ingersoll House, Dalamare Road, Cheshunt,
Herts EN8 9ND
Card mounts.

Impress Cards & Craft Materials
Slough Farm, Westhall, Halesworth, Suffolk IP19 8RN
Card mounts.

The DMC Corporation
Port Kearney Bld, 10 South Kearney,
NJ 070732-0650, USA
Zweigart Aida, linen and stranded cotton.

Gay Bowles Sales Inc
PO Box 1060, Janesville,WI, USA

Anne Brinkley Designs Inc
761 Palmer Avenue, Holmdel, NJ 97733, USA

Ireland Needlecraft Pty Ltd
2-4 Keppel Drive, Hallam, Victoria 3803, Australia

DMC Needlecraft Pty
PO Box 317, Earlswood 2206, New South Wales
2204, Australia
Zweigart Aida, linen and stranded cotton.

Our Fantasy Designers

The following designers can be contacted at the addresses below:

Sue Cook at The August Moon Design Company Limited, 32 Wavell Drive, Malpas, Newport, Gwent NP20 6QN.
Website: www.augustmoon.co.uk.

Linda & Roger Garland at Lakeside Gallery, Fleardon Farm, Lezant, Launceston, Cornwall PL15 9NW.
Website www.lakeside-gallery.com

Susan Penny at Penny & Penny, 135 Bay View Road, Northam, Devon EX39 1BJ. email: penny.andpenny@virgin.net

Helen Philipps at Merry Heart Designs, PO Box 110, Hoylake, Wirral CH48 2WD. Website: www.merryheart.co.uk.

Pinn at Old Orchard Cottage, Knutsford Road, Antrobus, Northwich, Cheshire CW9 6JW. Website: www.x-stitch.co.uk

Mary Stockett, The Miranda Corporation. Website: www.webmiranda.com

Teresa Wentzler, TW Designworks. Website: www.twdesignworks.com

Acknowledgments

The publishers would like to thank the following people: Sue Cook, Maria Diaz, Susan Penny,
Saifhon Borisuthibundit and Rungrat Puthikul at Pinn, Mary Stockett, Teresa Wentzler for their design contributions;
Michaela Learner, Christine Thompson, Ann Swetman, Penn O'Gara for their expert stitching;
Doreen Holland for her chart checking;
Linda & Roger Garland for their art; and Susan and Martin Penny for producing the book.

Chart Index

Index

❦

Entries in *italics* indicates illustrations, **bold** indicates charts.